はしがき

　本書は第一学習社発行の英語教科書「Vivid English Communication III」に完全準拠したノートです。各パート見開き2ページで，主に教科書本文の予習や授業傍用での使用に役立つよう工夫しました。

CONTENTS

Lesson 1		4
Lesson 2		6
Lesson 3		12
Lesson 4		16
Lesson 5		20
Lesson 6		24
Lesson 7		28
Lesson 8		32
Lesson 9		36
Lesson 10		40
Lesson 11	No Rain, No Rainbow	44
Lesson 12	*Natto* Saves People in Need	50
Lesson 13	*Sazae-san* and Machiko Hasegawa	56
Lesson 14	A Lover of the Slums of Ghana	62
Lesson 15	To Achieve Gender Equality	68
Lesson 16	A World with No Fish	74
Lesson 17	Bats and Gloves Instead of Bombs and Guns	82
Lesson 18	"Brighten the World in Your Corner"	90
Lesson 19	Food Technology	98
Lesson 20	Transforming Our World	106

本書の構成と利用法

　本書は教科書本文を完全に理解するための学習の導きをしています。本書を最大限に活用して，教科書本文の理解を深めましょう。

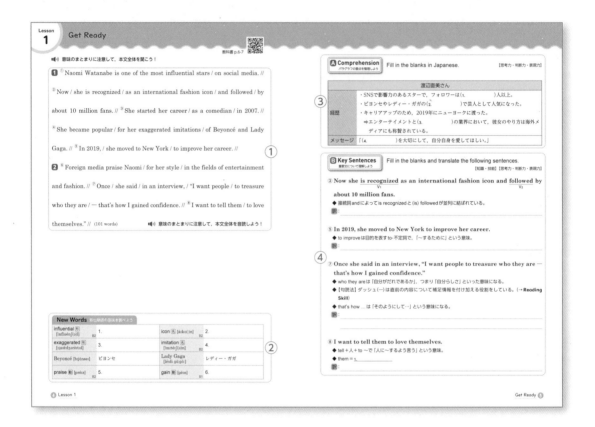

① 教科書本文

意味のまとまりごとにスラッシュ (/) を入れました。ここで示した意味のまとまりを意識しながら音読しましょう。また，学習がしやすいよう，一文ずつ番号を付けました。上部の二次元コードは，本文音声のリスニングや音読に使用できる「スピーキング・トレーナー」にリンクしています。右ページに詳しい解説があります。

② New Words

新出単語の意味を調べて，日本語で記入しましょう。単語の品詞と発音記号も示しました。A1〜B2は，CEFR-Jでのレベルを表します。A1 (易) 〜B2 (難) です。

『CEFR-J Wordlist Version 1.6』東京外国語大学投野由紀夫研究室. (URL: http://cefr-j.org/download.htmlより2021年2月ダウンロード)

③ **A Comprehension**

本文のまとめとなる図表を日本語で完成させることで本文の理解を深める問題です。パートごとにさまざまな形の図表を完成させます。

④ **B Key Sentences**

教科書の本文で，リーディングスキルに関連したものや，文構造が複雑なものや指示語を含むものなどを重要文と位置づけ，解説を加えました。解説を日本語や英語で完成させ，和訳をする問題です。日本語を補う問題の解答欄はカッコで，英語を補う問題の解答欄は下線で示しています。

スピーキング・トレーナー

本文の音声データ無料配信，音読用のボイスレコーダーが使用できます。
ブラウザ版とアプリ版 (iOS，Android) をご用意しています。
https://dg-w.jp/b/91e0021

本書の発行終了とともに当サイトを閉鎖することがあります。

アクセスキー 　　w6v4a

音声データ配信

音声をPCやスマートフォンなどから聞くことができます。（PCはブラウザ版のみ対応しています）

＊音声のダウンロードは，PCの場合はブラウザ版，スマートフォンの場合はアプリ版でご利用いただけます。アプリ版ではアプリ内でのみ再生が可能です。

＊アップしてある音声データは著作権法で保護されています。音声データの利用は個人が私的に利用する場合に限られます。データを第三者に提供・販売することはできません。

ボイスレコーダー

音読の学習効果をさらに高めるために，自分の発話の録音ができるボイスレコーダーを用意しました。PCやスマートフォンからご利用できます。

ボイスレコーダーの使用にはユーザーIDとパスワードが必要です。IDとパスワードを自分で設定 (半角英数字5文字以上) して，利用を開始してください。

メモ欄

ID	
パスワード	

＊IDとパスワードは紛失しないようにしてください。万が一紛失した場合は，それまでに記録された学習履歴がすべて参照できなくなります。復元はできませんので，ご注意ください。

＊音声データは各レッスンのページに個別に用意した二次元コードを読み取れば，ログインなしで聞くことができます。

＊正常に動作しない場合は「ヘルプ」→「動作要件」をご確認ください。

■情報料は無料ですが，通信費は利用者の負担となります。

■Wi-Fi環境でのご利用を推奨します。

■アプリ版では，教材データのダウンロード時と録音データのアップロード時等に通信が発生します。

教科書 p.6-7

◀)) 意味のまとまりに注意して，本文全体を聞こう！

1 ①Naomi Watanabe is one of the most influential stars / on social media. //

②Now / she is recognized / as an international fashion icon / and followed / by about 10 million fans. // ③She started her career / as a comedian / in 2007. //

④She became popular / for her exaggerated imitations / of Beyoncé and Lady Gaga. // ⑤In 2019, / she moved to New York / to improve her career. //

2 ⑥Foreign media praise Naomi / for her style / in the fields of entertainment and fashion. // ⑦Once / she said / in an interview, / "I want people / to treasure who they are / — that's how I gained confidence. // ⑧I want to tell them / to love themselves." //　(101 words)

◀)) 意味のまとまりに注意して，本文全体を音読しよう！

New Words 新出単語の意味を調べよう			
influential 形 [ìnfluénʃ(ə)l] B2	1.	icon 名 [áɪkɑ(:)n] B2	2.
exaggerated 形 [ɪgzǽdʒərèɪtɪd]	3.	imitation 名 [ìmɪtéɪʃ(ə)n] B2	4.
Beyoncé [bɪjánseɪ]	ビヨンセ	Lady Gaga [léɪdi gá:gà:]	レディー・ガガ
praise 動 [préɪz] B2	5.	gain 動 [géɪn] B1	6.

A Comprehension
パラグラフの要点を整理しよう

Fill in the blanks in Japanese.

【思考力・判断力・表現力】

渡辺直美さん	
経歴	・SNSで影響力のあるスターで，フォロワーは(1.　　　　　　)人以上。 ・ビヨンセやレディー・ガガの(2.　　　　　　)で芸人として人気になった。 ・キャリアアップのため，2019年にニューヨークに渡った。 ➡エンターテイメントと(3.　　　　　)の業界において，彼女のやり方は海外メディアにも称賛されている。
メッセージ	「(4.　　　　　)を大切にして，自分自身を愛してほしい。」

B Key Sentences
重要文について理解しよう

Fill in the blanks and translate the following sentences.

【知識・技能】【思考力・判断力・表現力】

② Now she <u>is recognized</u> as an international fashion icon and <u>followed</u> by
$\qquad$ V₁ $\qquad$ V₂

about 10 million fans.

◆ 接続詞andによってis recognizedと (is) followedが並列に結ばれている。

訳：_____

⑤ In 2019, she moved to New York to improve her career.

◆ to improveは目的を表すto-不定詞で，「～するために」という意味。

訳：_____

⑦ Once she said in an interview, "I want people to treasure who they are —
that's how I gained confidence."

◆ who they areは「自分がだれであるか」，つまり「自分らしさ」といった意味になる。

◆【句読法】ダッシュ（―）は直前の内容について補足情報を付け加える役割をしている。(→**Reading Skill**)

◆ that's how ...は「そのようにして…」という意味になる。

訳：_____

_____

⑧ I want to tell them to love themselves.

◆ tell＋人＋to ～で「人に～するよう言う」という意味。

◆ them = 1._____

訳：_____

教科書 p.8-9

■))) 意味のまとまりに注意して，本文全体を聞こう！

1 ①You may know / that some animals / ― koalas, kangaroos and wombats / ― are native to Australia. // ②But, / how about quokkas? // ③Thanks to their round cheeks and cute smiles, / they are called "the happiest animals on earth." //

2 ④Quokkas mainly live / on Rottnest Island / in the southwest / of the Australian mainland. // ⑤The name "Rottnest" / comes from the Dutch phrase / for "rat's nest." // ⑥When they were first discovered / by Dutch explorers / in the 17th century, / they were mistaken / for giant rats. //

3 ⑦Quokkas are such friendly creatures / that they approach tourists / for food. // ⑧However, / they are designated / as an endangered species, / so you are not allowed / to touch or feed them. // ⑨But don't be disappointed. // ⑩Just looking at their smiles / will make you happy. // (118 words)

■))) 意味のまとまりに注意して，本文全体を音読しよう！

New Words 新出単語の意味を調べよう			
native 形 [néɪtɪv] A2	1.	quokka 名 [kwákə]	2.
Rottnest [rá(:)tnest]	ロットネスト(島)	southwest 名 [sàʊθwést] B1	3.
mainland 名 [méɪnlənd]	4.	Dutch [dʌtʃ]	オランダ語の，オランダの
phrase 名 [fréɪz] B1	5.	explorer 名 [ɪksplɔ́:rər] B2	6.
giant 形 [dʒáɪənt] B1	7.	creature 名 [krí:tʃər] A2	8.
approach 動 [əpróʊtʃ] B2	9.	designate 動 [dézɪgnèɪt]	10.
endangered 形 [ɪndéɪn(d)ʒərd] A2	11.	species 名 [spí:ʃi:z] B2	12.
disappointed 形 [dìsəpóɪntɪd] A2	13.		

A Comprehension パラグラフの要点を整理しよう　Fill in the blanks in Japanese.　【思考力・判断力・表現力】

クオッカ
・(1.　　　　　　　)が丸く，笑顔がかわいく，人懐っこい。 ➡「世界一幸せな動物」と呼ばれている。 ・オーストラリア本土の(2.　　　　　　　)にあるロットネスト島に生息している。 ・17世紀に，(3.　　　　　　　)の探検家たちに最初に発見された。 ・絶滅危惧種に指定されており，触れたり(4.　　　　　　　)たりすることは禁止されている。

B Key Sentences 重要文について理解しよう　Fill in the blanks and translate the following sentences.
【知識・技能】【思考力・判断力・表現力】

① **You may know that some animals ― koalas, kangaroos and wombats ―
are native to Australia.**

　◆【句読法】ダッシュは直前の語句の具体例を導く役割をしている。(→ **Reading Skill**)

　◆ that-節内はS＋V＋Cの構造で，SとVの間にダッシュによる挿入があることに注意。

　訳：_____

　　　_____

⑥ **When they were first discovered by Dutch explorers in the 17th century,
they were mistaken for giant rats.**

　◆ they = 1._____

　◆ mistake A for Bで「AをBと間違える」という意味。ここではAを主語にした受け身になっている。

　訳：_____

　　　_____

⑦ **Quokkas are such friendly creatures that they approach tourists for
food.**

　◆ such (a) … that ～で「とても…なので～，～するほど…」という意味。suchの後には形容詞＋名詞がくる。

　訳：_____

⑩ **Just looking at their smiles will make you happy.**
　　　　　　　S　　　　　　　　　　　　　V　　　O　　C

　◆ S＋V＋O＋Cの文。make＋O＋Cで「OをCにする」という意味で，「O＝C」の関係になっている。

　訳：_____

教科書 p.10-11

🔊 意味のまとまりに注意して，本文全体を聞こう！

1 ①Do you know of Taro Okamoto, / who was one of the most famous Japanese artists? // ②As a painter, sculptor and writer, / he challenged traditional Japanese values. //

2 ③As a producer of Expo '70, / Okamoto created *the Tower of the Sun*, / a monument / overflowing with primitive power. // ④At that time, / it was severely criticized / by some artists / because it didn't seem to reflect / the traditional Japanese sense of beauty. // ⑤Yet, / such criticism didn't discourage him / at all. // ⑥He was an artist / with a consistent attitude / and strong beliefs. // ⑦Now / *the Tower of the Sun* is considered / one of his most outstanding works. // (100 words)

🔊 意味のまとまりに注意して，本文全体を音読しよう！

New Words 新出単語の意味を調べよう			
sculptor 名 [skʌ́lptər]	1.	expo 名 [ékspou]	2.
overflow 動 [òuvərflóu]	3.	primitive 形 [prímətɪv] B1	4.
severely 副 [sɪvíərli] B1	5.	criticize 動 [krítəsàɪz] A2	6.
reflect 動 [rɪflékt] A2	7.	criticism 名 [krítəsìz(ə)m] B2	8.
discourage 動 [dɪskə́:rɪdʒ] B1	9.	consistent 形 [kənsíst(ə)nt] B2	10.

Comprehension
パラグラフの要点を整理しよう

Fill in the blanks in Japanese.

【思考力・判断力・表現力】

岡本太郎	
・最も有名な日本人(1.　　　　　　)の一人。画家，彫刻家，作家。	
・日本の(2.　　　　　　)な価値観に異議を唱えた。	
『太陽の塔』	・1970年の万博のために作られた，原始的な力にあふれたモニュメント。
	・日本の伝統的な(3.　　　　　　)を反映していないとして批判された。
	・岡本は批判にめげず，一貫した態度と強い(4.　　　　　　)を貫いた。

B Key Sentences
重要文について理解しよう

Fill in the blanks and translate the following sentences.

【知識・技能】【思考力・判断力・表現力】

③ As a producer of Expo '70, Okamoto created *the Tower of the Sun,* a monument overflowing with primitive power.

- ◆ a monument以下は *the Tower of the Sun* の追加説明で，同格の関係になっている。
- ◆ 現在分詞overflowing以下がa monumentを後ろから修飾している。

訳 :

④ At that time, it was severely criticized by some artists because it didn't seem to reflect the traditional Japanese sense of beauty.

- ◆【指示語の指す内容】At that timeは「(『太陽の塔』が制作された)当時」を指し，2つのitは 1.
　　　　　　　　　　　　　　　　　を指す。(→ **Reading Skill**)

訳 :

⑤ Yet, such criticism didn't discourage him at all.

- ◆ yetは，前文の内容に対して「しかしながら，けれども」という逆接の意味を表す。

訳 :

⑥ He was an artist with a consistent attitude and strong beliefs.

- ◆ withは「…を持った」という所持・所有を表す。

訳 :

🔊 意味のまとまりに注意して，本文全体を聞こう！

1 ① Gitanjali Rao was selected / as *TIME*'s 2020 "Kid of the Year" / at the age of 15. // ② The Indian-American scientist and inventor / uses technology / to solve social and environmental problems. //

2 ③ For example, / Gitanjali invented an AI-based service / called "Kindly." // ④ It detects words / that could be related to cyberbullying. // ⑤ She also created "Tethys," / a device / that can identify lead contamination / in drinking water. //

3 ⑥ Her mission doesn't stop there. // ⑦ Gitanjali has also held innovative workshops / on STEM / globally. // ⑧ With these workshops, / she intends to create a global community / of young innovators / to tackle world problems. // ⑨ She says, / "It's never too early / to start making a difference. // ⑩ Every one of us / has the power / to change the world." // (114 words)

🔊 意味のまとまりに注意して，本文全体を音読しよう！

New Words 新出単語の意味を調べよう			
Gitanjali Rao [gɪtǽndʒəli ráʊ]	ギタンジャリ・ラオ	inventor 名 [ɪnvéntər] B2	1.
detect 動 [dɪtékt] B2	2.	cyberbullying 名 [sáɪbərbùlɪŋ]	3.
Tethys [tíːθɪs]	テティス	identify 動 [aɪdéntəfàɪ] B2	4.
contamination 名 [kəntæmɪnéɪʃ(ə)n]	5.	mission 名 [míʃ(ə)n] B1	6.
innovative 形 [ínəvèɪtɪv] B2	7.	STEM [stém]	=Science, Technology, Engineering and Mathematics
intend 動 [ɪnténd] B1	8.	innovator 名 [ínəvèɪtər] B1	9.
tackle 動 [tǽk(ə)l] B2	10.		

A Comprehension
パラグラフの要点を整理しよう

Fill in the blanks in Japanese.

【思考力・判断力・表現力】

ギタンジャリ・ラオさん	
・インド系アメリカ人の科学者であり(1.　　　　　)である。	
・15歳のとき，『タイム』誌の「キッド・オブ・ザ・イヤー」に選ばれた。	
発明・取り組み	・「Kindly」…AIを利用してネットいじめに関連する(2.　　　　　)を検出するサービス。 ・「Tethys」…飲料水の(3.　　　　　)汚染を探知する装置。 ・世界各地でSTEMに関する革新的な(4.　　　　　)を開催している。

B Key Sentences
重要文について理解しよう

Fill in the blanks and translate the following sentences.

【知識・技能】【思考力・判断力・表現力】

④ **It detects words that could be related to cyberbullying.**

◆【指示語の指す内容】It = 1.＿＿＿＿＿＿＿＿＿＿＿＿＿＿＿＿＿（→ **Reading Skill**)

◆ couldは「〜しうる，〜かもしれない」という可能性を表す。

訳：..

⑥ **Her mission doesn't stop there.**

◆ thereは具体的には，テクノロジーを駆使して諸問題を解決するものを発明するという活動の場を指す。

訳：..

⑧ **With these workshops, she intends to create a global community of young innovators to tackle world problems.**

◆ withは「…で，…を使って」という意味で，道具・手段を表す用法。

◆ intend to 〜は「(2.　　　　　　　　　　　　　　　)」の意味。

訳：..

....

⑨ **She says, "It's never too early to start making a difference."**

◆ it's never too early to 〜は「〜するのに早すぎるということは決してない」の意味。

◆ make a differenceは「変化をもたらす，違いを生じさせる」の意味。

訳：..

Get Ready

■)) 意味のまとまりに注意して，本文全体を聞こう！

1 ①Look at these pictures. // ②They all have the "golden ratio" / in them. // ③The golden ratio is a mathematical ratio / of 1:1.618. //

2 ④It is said / that many famous architectural works, / artworks / and other objects / have been composed / with this ratio. // ⑤For example, / the Pyramids of Giza in Egypt, / the Parthenon in Athens, / and Kinkakuji Temple in Kyoto / are among them. //

3 ⑥Why are people attracted / to these structures? // ⑦It may be / because the golden ratio is a kind of law / and order of nature. // ⑧We can also find the golden ratio / in beautiful objects / in nature, / such as flowers, / ferns / and seashells. // ⑨When we see objects / with this ratio, / we instinctively feel / that they are well-balanced, / pleasing / and beautiful. // (117 words)

■)) 意味のまとまりに注意して，本文全体を音読しよう！

New Words 新出単語の意味を調べよう			
golden 形 [góʊld(ə)n] A2	1.	ratio 名 [réɪʃiou]	2.
mathematical 形 [mæ̀θəmǽtɪk(ə)l] B2	3.	architectural 形 [ɑ̀ːrkɪtéktʃ(ə)r(ə)l]	4.
compose 動 [kəmpóʊz] B1	5.	pyramid 名 [pírəmɪd]	6.
Giza [gíːzə]	ギザ	Parthenon [pɑ́ːrθənɑ̀(ː)n]	パルテノン神殿
Athens [ǽθɪnz]	アテネ	fern 名 [fə́ːrn]	7.
seashell 名 [síːʃèl]	8.	instinctively 副 [ɪnstíŋ(k)tɪvli]	9.
well-balanced 形 [wèlbǽlənst] B2	10.	pleasing 形 [plíːzɪŋ] A2	11.

黄金比 …1:1.618という数学的な比率		
例	①有名な建築物や芸術作品 …エジプトのギザの(1.　　　　　)，アテネのパルテノン神殿，京都の金閣寺など ②自然界の美しいもの …花やシダ，(2.　　　　　)など	
黄金比を含むものを見ると，(3.　　　　　)的に心地よく美しいと感じる。	➡黄金比が自然界の法則や(4.　　　　　)の一種だからかもしれない。	

B **Key Sentences**
重要文について理解しよう

Fill in the blanks and translate the following sentences.

【知識・技能】【思考力・判断力・表現力】

④ **It is said that many famous architectural works, artworks and other objects have been composed with this ratio.**

◆ It is said that ＋ S ＋ V で「S は V だと言われている」という意味。

訳：_____

_____

⑤ **For example, the Pyramids of Giza in Egypt, the Parthenon in Athens, and Kinkakuji Temple in Kyoto are among them.**

◆【つなぎの語句 (例示)】For example によって，前文で述べられた建築物や芸術作品の (1.　　　　　) が導かれている。(→ **Reading Skill**)

訳：_____

_____

⑧ **We can also find the golden ratio in beautiful objects in nature, such as flowers, ferns and seashells.**

◆ such as 以下は，直前の beautiful objects in nature の具体例を表している。

訳：_____

⑨ **When we see objects with this ratio, we instinctively feel that they are well-balanced, pleasing and beautiful.**
$\underset{\text{S}}{\text{we}}$ $\underset{\text{V}}{\text{feel}}$ $\underset{\text{O}}{\text{that they are}}$

◆ 主節は S ＋ V ＋ O の文で，that-節中は S ＋ V ＋ C の構造になっている。

訳：_____

教科書 p.16-17

🔊 意味のまとまりに注意して，本文全体を聞こう！

1 ①Have you ever heard / of "ethical consumption"? // ②It means / to choose products or services / in consideration of the environment, / human rights, / or animal welfare. //

2 ③How can we become ethical consumers? // ④For example, / we can choose ethical products / such as fair-trade, eco-friendly or recycled products. // ⑤When shopping, / it is important / to consider / how the products were produced / before buying them. // ⑥Choosing ethical products / can help to improve our society. //

3 ⑦We can also help to save the environment / by installing solar panels / or choosing electric appliances / with low power consumption. // ⑧The time is just around the corner / when it will be normal / to live as an ethical consumer. //　(106 words)　🔊 意味のまとまりに注意して，本文全体を音読しよう！

New Words 新出単語の意味を調べよう		
ethical 形 [éθɪk(ə)l]	1.	
consideration 名 [kənsìdəréɪʃ(ə)n] B1	3.	
install 動 [ɪnstɔ́ːl] B1	5.	
appliance 名 [əpláɪəns]	7.	

consumption 名 [kənsʌ́m(p)ʃ(ə)n] B1	2.	
consumer 名 [kənsjúːmər] B1	4.	
electric 形 [ɪléktrɪk] A2	6.	

Fill in the blanks in Japanese.　【思考力・判断力・表現力】

エシカル消費	
…環境や（1.　　　　　　　　），動物福祉に配慮した製品やサービスを選ぶこと。	
例	・フェアトレード製品や環境に優しい製品，（2.　　　　　　　　）製品などを選ぶ。 ・買う前に商品がどのように作られたかを考える。 ・ソーラーパネルを設置したり，（3.　　　　　　　　）の少ない電化製品を選ぶ。

↓

エシカルな商品を選ぶことはよりよい（4.　　　　　　　　）につながる。

Fill in the blanks and translate the following sentences.
【知識・技能】【思考力・判断力・表現力】

④ For example, we can choose ethical products such as fair-trade, eco-friendly or recycled products.

◆【つなぎの語句（例示）】such as が直前の 1.＿＿＿＿＿＿＿＿＿＿ の具体例を導いている。

（→ **Reading Skill**）

訳：＿＿＿＿＿＿＿＿＿＿＿＿＿＿＿＿＿＿＿＿＿＿＿＿＿＿＿＿＿

＿＿＿＿＿＿＿＿＿＿＿＿＿＿＿＿＿＿＿＿＿＿＿＿＿＿＿＿＿

⑤ When shopping, it is important to consider how the products were produced before buying them.

◆ it は形式主語で，to 以下の内容を指している。
◆ how 以下の疑問詞節が consider の目的語になっている。

訳：＿＿＿＿＿＿＿＿＿＿＿＿＿＿＿＿＿＿＿＿＿＿＿＿＿＿＿＿＿

⑦ We can also help to save the environment by installing solar panels or choosing electric appliances with low power consumption.

◆ by ～ing で「～することによって」の意味。installing … と choosing … が or によって並列されている。

訳：＿＿＿＿＿＿＿＿＿＿＿＿＿＿＿＿＿＿＿＿＿＿＿＿＿＿＿＿＿

＿＿＿＿＿＿＿＿＿＿＿＿＿＿＿＿＿＿＿＿＿＿＿＿＿＿＿＿＿

⑧ The time is just around the corner when it will be normal to live as an ethical consumer.

◆ when は関係副詞で，when 以下が先行詞 The time を修飾している。先行詞と関係詞節が離れている形。

訳：＿＿＿＿＿＿＿＿＿＿＿＿＿＿＿＿＿＿＿＿＿＿＿＿＿＿＿＿＿

教科書 p.18-19

◀)) 意味のまとまりに注意して，本文全体を聞こう！

1 ①Do you know / there are some jungle schools / for orangutans? // ②These unique schools / to protect them / are located / in a jungle / in Borneo, / Indonesia. //

2 ③The orangutans / at these schools / have been left orphans. // ④They can't live / in the real wilderness / without first being taught survival skills / by humans. // ⑤That's why they are learning / how to build sturdy nests, / how to crack coconuts, / and even how to climb trees. //

3 ⑥Orangutans are losing their homes / because their rainforest habitat / is being destroyed / due to human activities / such as plantation development / and illegal deforestation. // ⑦As a result, / they are in danger of extinction. // ⑧What do you think / about the selfishness / of human beings? // (110 words)

◀)) 意味のまとまりに注意して，本文全体を音読しよう！

New Words 新出単語の意味を調べよう			
orangutan 名 [ɔːrǽŋətæ̀n]	1.	Borneo [bɔ́ːrniòʊ]	ボルネオ島
orphan 名 [ɔ́ːrf(ə)n] A2	2.	wilderness 名 [wíldərnəs] B2	3.
survival 名 [sərváɪv(ə)l] B1	4.	sturdy 形 [stə́ːrdi]	5.
crack 動 [krǽk] B2	6.	coconut 名 [kóʊkənʌ̀t] B2	7.
illegal 形 [ɪlíːg(ə)l] A2	8.	selfishness 名 [sélfɪʃnəs]	9.

Ⓐ Comprehension
パラグラフの要点を整理しよう

Fill in the blanks in Japanese.　　　　　【思考力・判断力・表現力】

人間
人間の活動や行動…プランテーション開発や違法な(1.　　　　　)
オランウータンのための(4.　　　　　)を作り，生き残る術を教える

オランウータン
オランウータンの生息地である(2.　　　　　)の破壊，住処の消失→(3.　　　　　)の危機
→孤児の出現

Ⓑ Key Sentences
重要文について理解しよう

Fill in the blanks and translate the following sentences.
【知識・技能】【思考力・判断力・表現力】

④ **They can't live in the real wilderness without first being taught survival skills by humans.**

◆ can't … without 〜ing「〜せずには…することができない」という二重否定の表現。

◆ being taughtは動名詞の受動態で，「教わること」という意味。

訳:

⑤ **That's why they are learning how to build sturdy nests, how to crack coconuts, and even how to climb trees.**

◆ that's why …は，前文の内容を受けて「(1.　　　　　)」という「結果」を導く表現。

(→ **Reading Skill**)

訳:

⑥ **Orangutans are losing their homes because their rainforest habitat is**
　　　　　　　　　　　　　　結果 ◆━━━ 原因
being destroyed due to human activities such as plantation development
　　　　　　　結果 ◆━━━ 原因
and illegal deforestation.

◆【つなぎの語句 (原因・結果)】becauseとdue toはどちらも「原因」を導く表現。(→ **Reading Skill**)

◆ is being destroyedは進行形の受動態で，「破壊されつつある」という意味。

訳:

教科書 p.20-21

■)) 意味のまとまりに注意して，本文全体を聞こう！

1 ① "One Team" was Japan's slogan / for the 2019 Rugby World Cup. // ② Sixteen of Japan's 31 players / were born / in other nations. // ③ The unity / shown by these players / of different backgrounds / surely moved the public. //

2 ④ Captain Michael Leitch, / a New Zealand-born Japanese, / created various opportunities / for the foreign-born players / to learn about Japan. // ⑤ For example, / he held quiz events / to teach them / about the country's history. // ⑥ Michael said, / "If they learn more / about Japan, / we can become even more united / as one team." //

3 ⑦ The team can be seen / as a mirror / of today's Japan. // ⑧ Many people / from diverse backgrounds / are gradually becoming part of Japanese society. // ⑨ As a result, / the diversity / they bring / can help Japan build a new era. // (119 words)

■)) 意味のまとまりに注意して，本文全体を音読しよう！

New Words 新出単語の意味を調べよう			
slogan 名 [slóʊɡ(ə)n] B1	1.	unity 名 [júːnəti]	2.
Michael Leitch [máɪk(ə)l líːtʃ]	リーチマイケル	unite 動 [junáɪt] B1	3.
diverse 形 [dəvə́ːrs] B1	4.	diversity 名 [dəvə́ːrsəti]	5.

Ⓐ Comprehension
パラグラフの要点を整理しよう

Fill in the blanks in Japanese.

【思考力・判断力・表現力】

2019年ラグビーワールドカップの日本代表チーム	
・メンバーの約(1.　　　　　　　)が外国出身であった。	
・スローガン「ワンチーム」のもと，チームの(2.　　　　　　　)が国民を感動させた。	
今日の日本社会 との共通点	日本代表チームは今日の日本を映す(3.　　　　　　　)である。 → 今日の日本：さまざまな背景を持つ多くの人々が，日本社会の構成員になろ うとしている。この(4.　　　　　　　)が日本が新時代を開くのに貢献する。

Ⓑ Key Sentences
重要文について理解しよう

Fill in the blanks and translate the following sentences.

【知識・技能】【思考力・判断力・表現力】

③ The unity shown by these players of different backgrounds surely moved the public.

　◆ 過去分詞shown以下がThe unityを後ろから修飾している。この部分全体が文の主語になっている。

　訳：＿＿＿＿＿＿＿＿＿＿＿＿＿＿＿＿＿＿＿＿＿＿＿＿＿＿＿＿＿＿＿＿＿＿＿

④ Captain Michael Leitch, a New Zealand-born Japanese, created various opportunities for the foreign-born players to learn about Japan.

　◆ コンマで挟まれた部分 (a New Zealand-born Japanese) は，Captain Michael Leitchの追加説明で，同格の関係になっている。

　訳：＿＿＿＿＿＿＿＿＿＿＿＿＿＿＿＿＿＿＿＿＿＿＿＿＿＿＿＿＿＿＿＿＿＿＿

　　＿＿＿＿＿＿＿＿＿＿＿＿＿＿＿＿＿＿＿＿＿＿＿＿＿＿＿＿＿＿＿＿＿＿＿

⑦ The team can be seen as a mirror of today's Japan.

　◆ be seen as ... はsee A as B「AをBとみなす」の受動態で，「…と（して）みなされる」の意味。

　訳：＿＿＿＿＿＿＿＿＿＿＿＿＿＿＿＿＿＿＿＿＿＿＿＿＿＿＿＿＿＿＿＿＿＿＿

⑨ As a result, the diversity they bring can help Japan build a new era.

　◆【つなぎの語句（原因・結果）】as a resultは，前文の内容を受けて「(1.　　　　　　　)」という「結果」を導いている。(→ **Reading Skill**)

　◆ they bringがthe diversityを後ろから修飾している。関係代名詞which [that] が省略されている。

　◆ they = 2.＿＿＿＿＿＿＿＿＿＿＿＿＿＿＿＿＿＿＿＿＿＿＿＿＿＿＿＿＿

　◆ help＋O＋動詞の原形は「Oが～するのに役立つ」の意味。

　訳：＿＿＿＿＿＿＿＿＿＿＿＿＿＿＿＿＿＿＿＿＿＿＿＿＿＿＿＿＿＿＿＿＿＿＿

Get Ready

教科書 p.22-23

🔊 意味のまとまりに注意して，本文全体を聞こう！

1 ①Everyone hopes to be healthy / and live a long life. // ②Will it ever be possible / for humans / to gain immortality, / then? //

2 ③Researchers hold different views / on this question. // ④Some argue / that everlasting life will be possible / in the future, / while others think / it's unlikely. // ⑤However, / many of them seem to agree / that we can delay aging. // ⑥One of the key factors / is to activate our "longevity genes." // ⑦This could be made possible, / for example, / by reducing our calorie intake. // ⑧The activated genes / could help damaged cells recover. // ⑨Moreover, / they might also prevent some serious diseases. //

3 ⑩Extending our life span / may lead to great changes / in our society. // ⑪People might retire / at the age of 85, / or centenarian athletes might even take part in the Olympics! // (125 words)

🔊 意味のまとまりに注意して，本文全体を音読しよう！

New Words 新出単語の意味を調べよう			
immortality 名 [ìmɔːrtǽləti] B2	1.	researcher 名 [rɪsə́ːrtʃər] B1	2.
argue 動 [áːrgjuː] A2	3.	everlasting 形 [èvərlǽstɪŋ] B2	4.
unlikely 形 [ʌnláɪkli] B1	5.	factor 名 [fǽktər] B2	6.
activate 動 [ǽktɪvèɪt]	7.	longevity 名 [lɑ(ː)ndʒévəti]	8.

calorie 名 [kǽləri]	9.	intake 名 [íntèɪk]	10.
cell 名 [sél] B1	11.	recover 動 [rɪkʌ́vər] B1	12.
extend 動 [ɪksténd] B1	13.	span 名 [spǽn]	14.
retire 動 [rɪtáɪər] A2	15.	centenarian 形 [sènt(ə)néəriən]	16.

A Comprehension
パラグラフの要点を整理しよう

Fill in the blanks in Japanese.　　　　　　　【思考力・判断力・表現力】

不老不死や長寿の可能性
不死は実現可能か？—(1.　　　　　　)を遅らせることは可能だと，多くの研究者は考えている。

⬆

> 長寿遺伝子を(2.　　　　　　)すること
> ⇒ダメージを受けた(3.　　　　　　)を回復させたり，深刻な
> (4.　　　　　　)を予防できる可能性がある。

B Key Sentences
重要文について理解しよう

Fill in the blanks and translate the following sentences.
【知識・技能】【思考力・判断力・表現力】

④ **Some argue that everlasting life will be possible in the future, while others think it's unlikely.**

◆ Some とは Some 1.　　　　　　　 のこと。

◆【つなぎの語句（対比・対照）】ここでは接続詞の 2.　　　　　　 によって2つの意見が対比されている。（→ **Reading Skill**）

訳 : ....

⑦ **This could be made possible, for example, by reducing our calorie intake.**

◆ This = to 3.　　　　　　　　　　　　　

◆ make＋O＋C「OをCにする」が受け身になった形。

◆ 具体例を表す for example が文中に挿入されている。

訳 : ....

⑩ **Extending our life span may lead to great changes in our society.**
　　　　　　S　　　　　　　　V

◆ 動名詞が主語になっている文。lead to ... は「…につながる」という意味。

訳 : ....

教科書 p.24-25

🔊 意味のまとまりに注意して，本文全体を聞こう！

①The train came out / of the long tunnel / into the snow country. //

■1 ②This is the opening passage / of the novel, / *Snow Country*, / written by Yasunari Kawabata. // ③This passage / in English / was translated / by Edward George Seidensticker, / an American scholar / of Japanese literature. // ④Compared with the original, / how is his translation different? //

■2 ⑤The sentence / in the Japanese original / has no explicit subject. // ⑥On the other hand, / Seidensticker translated the sentence / by using "the train" / as the subject. // ⑦Unlike Japanese, / subjects are usually required / in English. //

■3 ⑧In addition, / in the English version, / the scenery is described objectively / with a view / from the sky, / while it is viewed subjectively / from inside the train / in the Japanese original. // ⑨In this way, / if we compare Japanese novels / with their English translations, / we can observe their different ways / of seeing the world. // (136 words)

🔊 意味のまとまりに注意して，本文全体を音読しよう！

New Words 新出単語の意味を調べよう

tunnel 名 [tʌ́n(ə)l] B2	1.	novel 名 [nɑ́(:)v(ə)l] A2	2.
Edward George Seidensticker [édwərd dʒɔ́ːrdʒ sáɪdənstìkər]	エドワード・ジョージ・サイデンステッカー	scholar 名 [skɑ́(:)lər] B1	3.
literature 名 [lít(ə)rətʃər] B1	4.	explicit 形 [ɪksplísɪt]	5.
scenery 名 [síːn(ə)ri] A2	6.	objectively 副 [əbdʒéktɪvli]	7.
subjectively 副 [səbdʒéktɪvli]	8.	observe 動 [əbzɔ́ːrv] B1	9.

A Comprehension
パラグラフの要点を整理しよう

Fill in the blanks in Japanese.　　　【思考力・判断力・表現力】

『雪国』の原作と英訳の比較		
違い①	(1.　　　　　　　)の有無による違い	
	・原作：明示された主語はない。	
	・英訳：主語が必要。(2.　　　　　　　　　)が主語になっている。	
違い②	描写方法の違い	
	・原作：景色が列車の中から描写されている。…(3.　　　　　)的描写	
	・英訳：景色が空から描写されている。…(4.　　　　)的描写	

B Key Sentences
重要文について理解しよう

Fill in the blanks and translate the following sentences.

【知識・技能】【思考力・判断力・表現力】

② This is the opening passage of the novel, *Snow Country*, written by Yasunari Kawabata.

◆ written 以下は the novel を後置修飾している。間に the novel と同格の *Snow Country* が挿入されている。

訳：

④ Compared with the original, how is his translation different?

◆ Compared with ... は過去分詞の分詞構文。主語は，主節の主語と同じ 1.＿＿＿＿＿＿＿＿＿ であると考える。

訳：

⑧ In addition, in the English version, the scenery is described objectively with a view from the sky, while it is viewed subjectively from inside the train in the Japanese original.

◆ it = 2.＿＿＿＿＿＿＿＿＿＿＿

◆【つなぎの語句（対比・対照）】接続詞 while は，文の前半と後半の対比を表している。(→**Reading Skill**)

訳：

Get Ready

教科書 p.26-27

🔊 意味のまとまりに注意して，本文全体を聞こう！

1 ①Keisuke Honda is a well-known professional soccer player. // ②In 2010, / Keisuke was in South Africa / to play in the World Cup. // ③He visited an orphanage, / where he saw many miserable children. // ④This experience made him / aware of what he could do / to make the world a better place. //

2 ⑤Now, / as an entrepreneur, / Keisuke is trying hard / to offer people opportunities / to pursue their dreams. // ⑥First of all, / he established soccer schools / inside and outside Japan. // ⑦Next, / he set up funds / with famous and distinguished people / all over the world. // ⑧As a gifted and talented person, / he is conscious of his mission / to give people in need / a path to success. // (110 words)

🔊 意味のまとまりに注意して，本文全体を音読しよう！

New Words 新出単語の意味を調べよう			
orphanage 名 [ɔ́:rf(ə)nɪdʒ]	1.	miserable 形 [míz(ə)rəb(ə)l] B1	2.
aware 形 [əwéər] B1	3.	entrepreneur 名 [ɑ̀:ntrəprəná:r] B2	4.
pursue 動 [pərsjú:] A2	5.	distinguished 形 [dɪstíŋgwɪʃt] B2	6.
talented 形 [tǽləntɪd] B1	7.	conscious 形 [kɑ́(:)nʃəs] B1	8.

A Comprehension
パラグラフの要点を整理しよう

Fill in the blanks in Japanese.

【思考力・判断力・表現力】

本田圭佑選手の取り組み	
サッカー選手として	・2010年，ワールドカップでプレーするために南アフリカに行った。 →(1.　　　　　　)を訪れ，世界のために自分に何ができるか気づいた。
起業家として	・日本の国内外に(2.　　　　　　)スクールを設立した。 ・世界中の著名人と協力して(3.　　　　　　)を立ち上げた。
才能に恵まれた人間として	・困っている人々に(4.　　　　　　)への道を用意することが自分の使命だと考えている。

B Key Sentences
重要文について理解しよう

Fill in the blanks and translate the following sentences.

【知識・技能】【思考力・判断力・表現力】

④ <u>This experience</u> <u>made</u> <u>him</u> <u>aware</u> of what he could do to make the world
  S   V O C

 a better place.

 ◆ This experienceとは，孤児院で多くの不幸な (1.　　　　　　) と出会った経験を指す。

 ◆ S＋V＋O＋Cの文。made him aware of ... で「彼に…を気づかせた」という意味。

訳：

⑥ First of all, he established soccer schools inside and outside Japan.

 ◆【つなぎの語句 (列挙)】first of all「まず第一に」は，本田圭佑選手の，人々に夢を追い求める機会を提供する取り組みの1つ目の例を導いている。(→ **Reading Skill**)

訳：

⑦ Next, he set up funds with famous and distinguished people all over the
 world.

 ◆【つなぎの語句 (列挙)】next「次に」は，前文の1つ目の例に続いて，2つ目の例を導いている。

(→ **Reading Skill**)

訳：

⑧ As a gifted and talented person, he is conscious of his mission to give
 people in need a path to success.

 ◆ to give以下はhis missionを修飾するto-不定詞の形容詞用法。

訳：

教科書 p.28-29

🔊 意味のまとまりに注意して，本文全体を聞こう！

1 ①VR (virtual reality) technology has been developing / in the field of entertainment. // ②The moment we put on head-mounted VR goggles, / we can dive into a virtual world / and become a hero or a heroine / in a game. //

2 ③In addition to entertainment, / VR technology has been applied / to other fields / as well. // ④First, / this technology is also used / in medical fields. // ⑤It is used / by surgeons / to rehearse complex operations. // ⑥Second, / teachers can apply this technology / to their classrooms. // ⑦In a geography class, / for example, / students can visit any place / on the globe / on a virtual field trip. // ⑧Third, / VR-based training is offered / to prepare against natural disasters. //

3 ⑨VR technology will surely keep on developing. // ⑩We can continue / to expect many surprising benefits / from it. // (124 words)

🔊 意味のまとまりに注意して，本文全体を音読しよう！

New Words 新出単語の意味を調べよう			
virtual 形 [və́:rtʃuəl] B1	1.	mounted 形 [máʊntɪd]	2.
goggle 名 [gá(:)g(ə)l]	3.	dive 動 [dáɪv] B1	4.
heroine 名 [hérouən]	5.	apply 動 [əpláɪ] A2	6.
surgeon 名 [sə́:rdʒ(ə)n] B1	7.	rehearse 動 [rɪhə́:rs]	8.
complex 形 [ká(:)mplèks] B1	9.	operation 名 [à(:)pəréɪʃ(ə)n] B1	10.
globe 名 [glóʊb] A2	11.		

A Comprehension
パラグラフの要点を整理しよう

Fill in the blanks in Japanese.

【思考力・判断力・表現力】

分野	VR技術の応用例
エンターテイメント	仮想空間の中で，（1.　　　　　　）の主人公になりきることができる。
医療	複雑な（2.　　　　　）の模擬演習をすることができる。
教育	地理の授業で，バーチャル（3.　　　　　）で学ぶことができる。
災害対策	（4.　　　　　）からの避難訓練をすることができる。

B Key Sentences
重要文について理解しよう

Fill in the blanks and translate the following sentences.

【知識・技能】【思考力・判断力・表現力】

② The moment we put on head-mounted VR goggles, we can dive into a
   <u>V1</u> (under dive)
   virtual world and become a hero or a heroine in a game.
   <u>V2</u> (under become)

◆ The moment ... はS＋Vを従え，「…するとすぐに」の意味になる。

◆ andは動詞のdiveと1.＿＿＿＿＿＿＿を結びつけている。

訳：
....
....

③ In addition to entertainment, VR technology has been applied to other
   fields as well.

◆ apply A to B「AをBに応用する」が完了形の受動態になった形。

◆ ... as wellは「…もまた」の意味。「エンターテイメント分野に加えて他の分野にも」ということ。

訳：
....
....

④ First, this technology is also used in medical fields.

◆【つなぎの語句（列挙）】VR技術が他の分野に応用されている例が列挙されている。first「第一に」によって1つ目の例が導かれている。（→**Reading Skill**）

訳：
....

⑦ In a geography class, for example, students can visit any place on the
   globe on a virtual field trip.

◆「(2.　　　　　　　)」という意味のfor exampleが文中に挿入されており，VR技術が教室で応用される例を説明している。

訳：
....
....

教科書 p.30-31

🔊 意味のまとまりに注意して，本文全体を聞こう！

1 ①With a boxfish on his head, / Sakana-kun often appears / on TV. // ②He is popular / for his cheerful personality. // ③Moreover, / he is respected / for his knowledge / of fish. //

2 ④As a child, / Sakana-kun liked fish. // ⑤He also liked drawing. // ⑥He was obsessed with drawing fish / and didn't study / at all. // ⑦His elementary school teacher asked his mother / to make him study. // ⑧But she answered, / "He really likes fish, / and I'm happy / with just the way he is." //

3 ⑨His childhood dream / was to become an ichthyology professor. // ⑩Though he failed to enter university, / he worked hard / and proved himself / in the ichthyology field. // ⑪Later, / he was invited / to join a university / as a visiting associate professor. // ⑫His consistent love for fish / enabled him to realize his dream. // (124 words)

🔊 意味のまとまりに注意して，**本文全体を音読しよう！**

New Words 新出単語の意味を調べよう			
boxfish 名 [bá(:)ksfìʃ]	1.	personality 名 [pə̀:rsənǽləti] A2	2.
knowledge 名 [ná(:)lɪdʒ] A2	3.	obsess 動 [əbsés] B2	4.
ichthyology 名 [ìkθiá(:)lədʒi]	5.	prove 動 [prú:v] B1	6.
associate 形 [əsóuʃiət]	7.		

A Comprehension
パラグラフの要点を整理しよう

Fill in the blanks in Japanese.　　　　　　　【思考力・判断力・表現力】

さかなクン	
・テレビ番組に多く出演し，明るい(1.　　　　　　)で人気である。	
・魚に関する知識で(2.　　　　　)を集めている。	
幼少期	・いつも魚の絵を描き，(3.　　　　　　)はまったくしなかった。
夢	・子供の頃の夢は，魚類学の(4.　　　　　)になることだった。 ➡大学受験には失敗するが，努力を重ね，のちに客員准教授として大学に招かれ，夢を叶えた。

B Key Sentences
重要文について理解しよう

Fill in the blanks and translate the following sentences.

【知識・技能】【思考力・判断力・表現力】

③ **Moreover, he is respected for his knowledge of fish.**

◆【つなぎの語句 (追加)】moreoverが，前文で述べられたさかなクンの情報に新しい情報を付け加えている。(→ **Reading Skill**)

訳:

⑧ **But she answered, "He really likes fish, and I'm happy with just the way he is."**

◆ the way ＋ S ＋ be-動詞「そのままのS，Sのあり方」という意味。justは副詞で，「ちょうど，まさに」といった強調を表す。

訳:

⑩ **Though he failed to enter university, he worked hard and proved himself in the ichthyology field.**
　　　　　　　　　　　　　　　　　　　　　　S　V₁　　　　　　　　V₂

◆ 接続詞though「…だが」は譲歩の副詞節を導き，主節は動詞1.　　　　　　と2.　　　　　　が並列されている。

訳:

⑫ **His consistent love for fish enabled him to realize his dream.**

◆ enable ＋ O ＋ to ～で「Oが～するのを可能にする」という意味。

訳:

教科書 p.32-33

🔊 意味のまとまりに注意して，本文全体を聞こう！

1 ①These are stairs / decorated like a piano. // ②We can actually make a piano-like sound / by stepping on the stairs. // ③This motivates us / to use the stairs / rather than the escalator. // ④Using the stairs / is not only fun / but also good / for our health. //

2 ⑤This transparent trash bin / allows us to see the garbage / inside it. // ⑥We are more likely to separate garbage properly; / otherwise we may look bad / to others / around us. // ⑦In addition, / we are more likely to follow the garbage separation rules / after seeing the garbage / already separated correctly. //

3 ⑧Just small artifices / like these / evoke behavioral changes / to solve personal or social problems. // ⑨They don't require high-tech devices / or lots of expense, / and they can change people's behaviors / for the better. // (123 words)

🔊 意味のまとまりに注意して，本文全体を音読しよう！

New Words 新出単語の意味を調べよう			
decorate 動 [dékərèɪt] B2	1.	motivate 動 [móʊtəvèɪt] B1	2.
escalator 名 [éskəlèɪtər] A2	3.	transparent 形 [trænspǽr(ə)nt] B2	4.
trash 名 [trǽʃ] B1	5.	bin 名 [bín] B1	6.
properly 副 [prá(:)pərli] B1	7.	separation 名 [sèpəréɪʃ(ə)n] B1	8.
correctly 副 [kəréktli] A2	9.	artifice 名 [ɑ́ːrtɪfɪs]	10.
evoke 動 [ɪvóʊk]	11.	behavioral 形 [bɪhéɪvjər(ə)l]	12.
high-tech 形 [hàɪték] B2	13.	expense 名 [ɪkspéns] B1	14.

A Comprehension
パラグラフの要点を整理しよう
Fill in the blanks in Japanese. 【思考力・判断力・表現力】

仕掛けの例①	ピアノのように装飾された階段
・踏むと実際にピアノのような音が出る。	
➡階段を使いたくなり，楽しいだけでなく(1.　　　　　)にもよい。	
仕掛けの例②	透明なごみ箱
・分別しないと(2.　　　　　)から悪く思われる。	
・正しく分別されたごみを見ると，その(3.　　　　　)に従いやすくなる。	
➡きちんと分別をする可能性が上がる。	
小さな仕掛けで人々の(4.　　　　　)を変え，個人的・社会的課題を解決できる。	

B Key Sentences
重要文について理解しよう
Fill in the blanks and translate the following sentences.
【知識・技能】【思考力・判断力・表現力】

③ **This motivates us to use the stairs rather than the escalator.**

◆ This は，階段を踏むと実際に (1.　　　　　　　　　　　　) ことを指す。

訳：..

⑥ **We are more likely to separate garbage properly; otherwise we may look bad to others around us.**

◆ セミコロンは，強い関係性のある2つの文をつなぐ接続詞の役割をしている。

訳：..

....

⑦ **In addition, we are more likely to follow the garbage separation rules after seeing the garbage already separated correctly.**

◆【つなぎの語句（追加）】in addition は「追加」を表すつなぎの語句で，透明なごみ箱の利点を付け加えている。(→ **Reading Skill**)

訳：..

....

⑧ **Just small artifices like these evoke behavioral changes to solve personal**
　　　　　　　　S　　　　　　　V　　　O
or social problems.

◆ S＋V＋Oの文。to solve ... は不定詞の形容詞用法で，behavioral changes を修飾している。

訳：..

教科書 p.34-35

🔊 意味のまとまりに注意して，本文全体を聞こう！

1 ① Anju Niwata / and Professor Hidenori Watanave / have been involved / in the "Rebooting Memories" project. // ② This project aims to inherit memories of war / by colorizing prewar and wartime black-and-white photos. // ③ These photos are colorized / based on AI technology / and conversations / with war survivors. //

2 ④ In 2017, / as a high school student, / Anju met a man / who had experienced war / and listened to his story. // ⑤ Soon after, / she learned / about colorization technology / in Watanave's workshop, / and then colorized his photos. // ⑥ Seeing the colorized photos, / Anju and the man / felt a sense of closeness / to the past events / in the photos. //

3 ⑦ These encounters led to their project. // ⑧ They colorized photos / of people's daily lives / during wartime: / a family / under cherry blossoms / and a couple / gazing at a burnt-out city. // ⑨ The people / in these photos / look alive, / as if they were actually in front of us. //　(141 words)

🔊 意味のまとまりに注意して，本文全体を音読しよう！

New Words 新出単語の意味を調べよう			
reboot 動 [rìːbúːt]	1.	inherit 動 [ɪnhérət] B2	2.
colorize 動 [kʌ́ləràɪz]	3.	prewar 形 [prìːwɔ́ːr]	4.
wartime 名 [wɔ́ːrtàɪm] B2	5.	base 動 [béɪs] B1	6.
colorization 名 [kʌ̀ləraɪzéɪʃ(ə)n]	7.	closeness 名 [klóʊsnəs]	8.
couple 名 [kʌ́p(ə)l] A2	9.	gaze 動 [géɪz]	10.

Fill in the blanks in Japanese.　　　　　　【思考力・判断力・表現力】

	「記憶の解凍」プロジェクト	
目的	(1.　　　　　　　)の記憶の継承	
手段	戦前・戦中の(2.　　　　　　　)のカラー化	
きっかけ	高校生だった庭田杏珠さんが，ある男性から戦争の(3.　　　　　)を聞いた。その後， (4.　　　　　　　)技術を学び，その男性の写真をカラー化した。	

B **Key Sentences**
重要文について理解しよう

Fill in the blanks and translate the following sentences.
【知識・技能】【思考力・判断力・表現力】

② This project aims to inherit memories of war by colorizing prewar and wartime black-and-white photos.

　◆【主題文と支持文】冒頭の主題文（①）で中心的話題（「記憶の解凍」プロジェクト）が提示され，それについての説明が展開される支持文が続いている。（→ **Reading Skill**）

　訳 :

③ These photos are colorized based on AI technology and conversations with war survivors.

　◆ These photos = 1.

　◆ based on … 「…に基づいて」 がare colorizedを修飾している。

　訳 :

⑥ Seeing the colorized photos, Anju and the man felt a sense of closeness to the past events in the photos.

　◆ Seeing the colorized photosは現在分詞の分詞構文である。

　訳 :

⑨ The people in these photos look alive, as if they were actually in front of us.
　　　　　　S　　　　　　　　　V　　C

　◆ S＋V＋Cの文。look＋Cは「Cのように見える」の意味。

　◆ as if＋仮定法過去の文で「まるで…であるかのように」の意味。

　訳 :

教科書 p.36-37

🔊 意味のまとまりに注意して，本文全体を聞こう！

1 ①The WHO officially declared the world / free of smallpox / in 1980. // ②This was the result / of a WHO global vaccination campaign. // ③Today, / smallpox is the only infectious disease / that humans have successfully eradicated. // ④No effective treatment / for smallpox / exists, / and this devastating disease / killed millions of people / in the past. //

2 ⑤There was a Japanese physician / who contributed to the global eradication / of smallpox. // ⑥He is Dr. Isao Arita. // ⑦He headed the WHO Smallpox Eradication Unit / from 1977 / to 1985. // ⑧He was awarded the Japan Prize / in 1988 / for this great contribution. // ⑨The victory / over smallpox / is considered / the most remarkable achievement / in the history of international public health. // (108 words)

🔊 意味のまとまりに注意して，本文全体を音読しよう！

New Words 新出単語の意味を調べよう			
officially 副 [əfíʃ(ə)li] B1	1.	smallpox 名 [smɔ́:lpɑ̀(:)ks]	2.
vaccination 名 [væksɪnéɪʃ(ə)n]	3.	successfully 副 [səksésf(ə)li] A2	4.
eradicate 動 [ɪrǽdɪkèɪt]	5.	treatment 名 [trí:tmənt] B1	6.
devastating 形 [dévəstèɪtɪŋ] B1	7.	eradication 名 [ɪræ̀dɪkéɪʃ(ə)n]	8.
unit 名 [júːnɪt] A2	9.	victory 名 [víkt(ə)ri] B1	10.
remarkable 形 [rɪmɑ́:rkəb(ə)l] B1	11.		

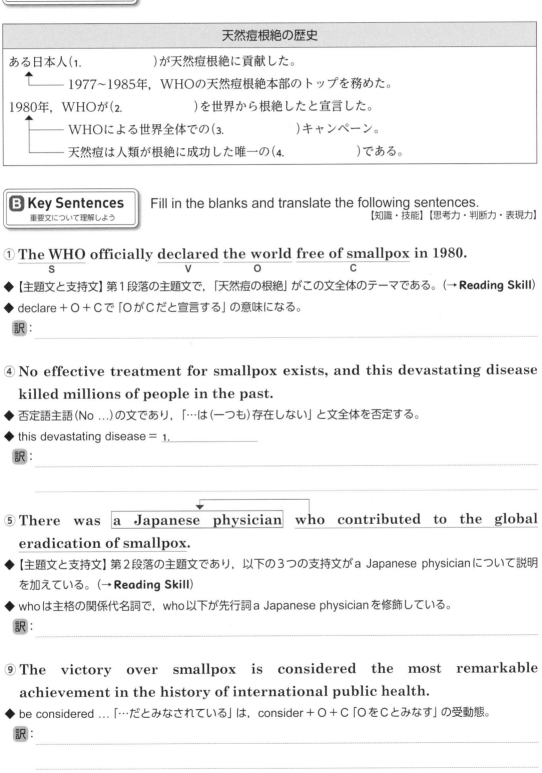

A Comprehension
パラグラフの要点を整理しよう

Fill in the blanks in Japanese.

【思考力・判断力・表現力】

天然痘根絶の歴史
ある日本人(1.　　　　　　　)が天然痘根絶に貢献した。 ┗━━ 1977~1985年，WHOの天然痘根絶本部のトップを務めた。 1980年，WHOが(2.　　　　　　　)を世界から根絶したと宣言した。 ┗━━ WHOによる世界全体での(3.　　　　　　)キャンペーン。 ┗━━ 天然痘は人類が根絶に成功した唯一の(4.　　　　　)である。

B Key Sentences
重要文について理解しよう

Fill in the blanks and translate the following sentences.
【知識・技能】【思考力・判断力・表現力】

① The WHO officially declared the world free of smallpox in 1980.
　　　S　　　　　　　　　V　　　　　　O　　　　　　C

◆【主題文と支持文】第1段落の主題文で，「天然痘の根絶」がこの文全体のテーマである。(→ **Reading Skill**)

◆ declare＋O＋Cで「OがCだと宣言する」の意味になる。

訳：_____

④ No effective treatment for smallpox exists, and this devastating disease killed millions of people in the past.

◆ 否定語主語(No ...)の文であり，「…は(一つも)存在しない」と文全体を否定する。

◆ this devastating disease ＝ 1._____

訳：_____

_____

⑤ There was a Japanese physician who contributed to the global eradication of smallpox.

◆【主題文と支持文】第2段落の主題文であり，以下の3つの支持文がa Japanese physicianについて説明を加えている。(→ **Reading Skill**)

◆ whoは主格の関係代名詞で，who以下が先行詞a Japanese physicianを修飾している。

訳：_____

⑨ The victory over smallpox is considered the most remarkable achievement in the history of international public health.

◆ be considered ...「…だとみなされている」は，consider＋O＋C「OをCとみなす」の受動態。

訳：_____

_____

教科書 p.38-39

◀)) 意味のまとまりに注意して，本文全体を聞こう！

1 ①Just walk down a busy street / and look around / to see what's happening. // ②You will find / that many people are glued / to their smartphones. // ③These people may need a digital detox. //

2 ④A digital detox means / to refrain / from using electronic devices / connected to the Internet, / such as smartphones and computers. // ⑤"Detoxing" from digital devices / is often seen / as a way / to focus on real-life social interactions / without distractions. //

3 ⑥You might feel anxious, / bored, / and even annoyed / without your smartphone / and other tech tools. // ⑦However, / a digital detox can be a rewarding experience / that will help / to rest your exhausted brain, / relieve social media fatigue, / and improve the quality of sleep. // ⑧Why don't you put down your digital devices sometimes / and be mindful / of your other activities and experiences? // (128 words)

◀)) 意味のまとまりに注意して，本文全体を音読しよう！

New Words 新出単語の意味を調べよう			
glue 動 [glúː]	1.	detox 名 [dìːtá(ː)ks]	2.
refrain 動 [rɪfréɪn]	3.	interaction 名 [ìnt(ə)rǽkʃ(ə)n] B1	4.
distraction 名 [dɪstrǽkʃ(ə)n] B2	5.	annoy 動 [ənɔ́ɪ] A2	6.
rewarding 形 [rɪwɔ́ːrdɪŋ]	7.	fatigue 名 [fətíːg]	8.
mindful 形 [máɪn(d)f(ə)l]	9.		

Fill in the blanks in Japanese.

【思考力・判断力・表現力】

デジタルデトックス		
概要	インターネットに接続されている(1.　　　　　　　)の使用を控えること　➡現実の社会的な(2.　　　　　　　)に集中する一つの方法	
効果	・疲れた(3.　　　　　)を休める。　　　・SNS疲れを和らげる。　・(4.　　　　　)の質を向上させる。	

B **Key Sentences**
重要文について理解しよう

Fill in the blanks and translate the following sentences.

【知識・技能】【思考力・判断力・表現力】

④ A digital detox means to refrain from using electronic devices connected to the Internet, such as smartphones and computers.

◆ 過去分詞で始まるconnected to the Internetがelectronic devicesを後置修飾している。

◆ such as ...は「…のような」の意味で，1.＿＿＿＿＿＿＿＿＿＿＿＿の具体例を導いている。

訳：＿＿＿＿＿＿＿＿＿＿＿＿＿＿＿＿＿＿＿＿＿＿＿＿＿＿＿＿＿＿＿＿＿

⑤ "Detoxing" from digital devices is often seen as a way to focus on real-life social interactions without distractions.

◆ "Detoxing"は動名詞で，"Detoxing" from digital devicesまでが主語になっている。

訳：＿＿＿＿＿＿＿＿＿＿＿＿＿＿＿＿＿＿＿＿＿＿＿＿＿＿＿＿＿＿＿＿＿

⑦ However, a digital detox can be a rewarding experience that will help to rest your exhausted brain, relieve social media fatigue, and improve the quality of sleep.

◆ thatは主格の関係代名詞で，that以下の節が先行詞a rewarding experienceを修飾している。

訳：＿＿＿＿＿＿＿＿＿＿＿＿＿＿＿＿＿＿＿＿＿＿＿＿＿＿＿＿＿＿＿＿＿

⑧ Why don't you put down your digital devices sometimes and be mindful of your other activities and experiences?

◆【未知語の推測】mindfulという単語は，mind「心」＋-ful「…に満ちた」という構造に注目すると，「気を配る，大切にしている」といった意味を推測することができる。(→ **Reading Skill**)

訳：＿＿＿＿＿＿＿＿＿＿＿＿＿＿＿＿＿＿＿＿＿＿＿＿＿＿＿＿＿＿＿＿＿

教科書 p.40-41

🔊 意味のまとまりに注意して，本文全体を聞こう！

1 ①A surprising amount of water / is used / in our daily lives. // ②The term "water footprint" / can be a good indicator / of this. // ③It refers to the amount of water / that is used and polluted / in order to produce the goods or services / we use. // ④A water footprint can be calculated / for any product. //

2 ⑤For instance, / a cup of coffee / needs 132 liters of water, / and one margherita pizza / requires 1,259 liters. // ⑥The water footprint / of one kilogram / of beef / is equal / to as much as 15,415 liters. // ⑦A pair of jeans / requires about 8,000 liters, / and one car requires 52,000−83,000 liters! //

3 ⑧It is important / to realize / that even though water is a limited resource, / we depend on it so much / in every aspect of our lives. // ⑨The water footprint helps visualize this fact. // (134 words)

🔊 意味のまとまりに注意して，本文全体を音読しよう！

New Words 新出単語の意味を調べよう			
term 名 [tə́:rm] B1	1.	footprint 名 [fútprìnt]	2.
indicator 名 [índɪkèɪtər]	3.	calculate 動 [kǽlkjəlèɪt] B1	4.
instance 名 [ínst(ə)ns] B1	5.	liter 名 [líːtər] A2	6.
margherita 名 [màːrgəríːtə]	7.	jean 名 [dʒíːn] A1	8.
aspect 名 [ǽspekt] B1	9.	visualize 動 [víʒu(ə)làɪz]	10.

A Comprehension
パラグラフの要点を整理しよう

Fill in the blanks in Japanese.

【思考力・判断力・表現力】

ウォーターフットプリントとは		
…製品やサービスを作るために使用されたり（1. 　　　　　）される水の量		
例	コーヒー 1杯：132リットル	ピザ1枚：1,259リットル
	（2.　　　　　）1kg：15,415リットル	ジーンズ1着：約（3.　　　　　）リットル
➡水は（4.　　　　　）資源であるのに，私たちは生活のあらゆるところで水に依存しているということを認識することが重要である。		

B Key Sentences
重要文について理解しよう

Fill in the blanks and translate the following sentences.

【知識・技能】【思考力・判断力・表現力】

② **The term "water footprint" can be a good indicator of this.**

◆【未知語の推測】footprintという単語は，foot「足」＋print「跡，痕跡」→「足跡」という意味を推測できる。water footprintという語句の意味は，後に続く文や具体例から推測できる。（→ **Reading Skill**）

訳：＿＿＿＿＿＿＿＿＿＿＿＿＿＿＿＿＿＿＿＿＿＿＿＿＿＿＿＿＿＿＿

③ **It refers to the amount of** water **that is used and polluted in order to produce** the goods or services **we use.**

◆ It ＝ 1.＿＿＿＿＿＿＿＿＿＿＿＿＿＿＿＿＿＿＿＿

◆ thatは主格の関係代名詞で，that以下の節が先行詞waterを修飾している。関係詞節中ではさらに，we useがthe goods or servicesを修飾している。

訳：＿＿＿＿＿＿＿＿＿＿＿＿＿＿＿＿＿＿＿＿＿＿＿＿＿＿＿＿＿＿＿

＿＿＿＿＿＿＿＿＿＿＿＿＿＿＿＿＿＿＿＿＿＿＿＿＿＿＿＿＿＿＿＿

⑥ **The water footprint of one kilogram of beef is equal to as much as 15,415 liters.**

◆ The water footprint of one kilogram of beefまでがこの文の主語になっている。

訳：＿＿＿＿＿＿＿＿＿＿＿＿＿＿＿＿＿＿＿＿＿＿＿＿＿＿＿＿＿＿＿

⑧ **It is important to realize that even though water is a limited resource, we depend on it so much in every aspect of our lives.**

◆ that以下全体がrealizeの目的語となっており，that-節の中にeven thoughが導く副詞節がある。

訳：＿＿＿＿＿＿＿＿＿＿＿＿＿＿＿＿＿＿＿＿＿＿＿＿＿＿＿＿＿＿＿

＿＿＿＿＿＿＿＿＿＿＿＿＿＿＿＿＿＿＿＿＿＿＿＿＿＿＿＿＿＿＿＿

教科書 p.42-43

🔊 意味のまとまりに注意して，本文全体を聞こう！

1 ①The Earth is surrounded / by countless pieces of waste / called "space debris." // ②They are parts / of abandoned rocket bodies / and satellites. // ③It is estimated / that there are more than 100 million pieces / of space debris / orbiting around the Earth. //

2 ④Space debris travels / at about eight kilometers / per second. // ⑤If it hits and damages satellites / used for climate research, / telecommunications / and navigation, / it will lead to serious consequences. //

3 ⑥Researchers have been studying ways / to remove space debris. // ⑦For example, / they have developed a remotely controlled vehicle / and a space net satellite / designed to capture debris. // ⑧However, / debris removal technology / has not yet been put into practical use. // ⑨Further international cooperation / will be necessary / for sustainable space development. // (116 words)

🔊 意味のまとまりに注意して，本文全体を音読しよう！

New Words 新出単語の意味を調べよう			
countless 形 [káʊntləs] B1	1.	abandoned 形 [əbǽnd(ə)nd] B2	2.
satellite 名 [sǽt(ə)làɪt] B1	3.	estimate 動 [éstɪmèɪt] B1	4.
orbit 動 [ɔ́:rbət]	5.	telecommunication 名 [tèləkəmjùːnɪkéɪʃ(ə)n] B1	6.
navigation 名 [nævɪgéɪʃ(ə)n] B2	7.	consequence 名 [ká(:)nsəkwèns] A2	8.
remotely 副 [rɪmóʊtli]	9.	removal 名 [rɪmúːv(ə)l]	10.
cooperation 名 [koʊɑ̀(:)pəréɪʃ(ə)n] B2	11.		

Comprehension パラグラフの要点を整理しよう

Fill in the blanks in Japanese.

【思考力・判断力・表現力】

宇宙ごみ	
…(1.　　　　　　)されたロケットや人工衛星の部品で，推定1億個以上が地球を周回している。	
問題点	宇宙ごみが気象衛星・通信衛星・航行衛星に(2.　　　　　　)すると，深刻な事態をもたらすことになる。
解決策	宇宙ごみ除去技術は研究・開発が進んでいるが，まだ(3.　　　　　　)されていない。 ➡持続可能な宇宙開発には，さらなる(4.　　　　　　)が必要である。

B **Key Sentences** 重要文について理解しよう

Fill in the blanks and translate the following sentences.

【知識・技能】【思考力・判断力・表現力】

③ It is estimated that there are more than 100 million pieces of space debris orbiting around the Earth.

◆ It is estimated that ... は「…だと推定されている」の意味で，It は that 以下の内容を受ける形式主語。

◆ There is ... ＋現在分詞で「…が〜している」という意味を表す。

訳：_____

_____

⑤ If it hits and damages satellites used for climate research, telecommunications and navigation, it will lead to serious consequences.

◆ 1つ目の it は 1._____ を指し，2つ目の it は先行する if-節の内容を受ける。

◆ 過去分詞の used 以下は satellites を後置修飾している。

訳：_____

_____

⑧ However, debris removal technology has not yet been put into practical use.

◆【事実と意見の区別】宇宙ごみの除去技術に関する客観的な「事実」を述べた文である。(→ **Reading Skill**)

◆ has not yet been put into ... は現在完了形の受動態の否定形である。

訳：_____

⑨ Further international cooperation will be necessary for sustainable space development.

◆【事実と意見の区別】will be necessary「必要となるだろう」という，書き手の主観的な「意見」を述べた文である。(→ **Reading Skill**)

訳：_____

_____

教科書 p.44-45

🔊 意味のまとまりに注意して，本文全体を聞こう！

1 ①In the animated movie, / *Tenkinoko* / (*Weathering with You*), / it continues to rain / for over two years, / and as a result / the city of Tokyo is changed a lot. // ②Could this actually happen / in real life? //

2 ③It's unlikely / that it would rain continuously / for so long. // ④In fact, / the annual precipitation of Tokyo / has barely changed at all / over the last thirty years. // ⑤On the other hand, / however, / it is a fact / that abnormal weather / such as heavy downpours / is becoming more frequent / in Japan. // ⑥There have been increasing cases / of heavy rainfall / causing serious damage. //

3 ⑦One of the factors / behind such abnormal weather / is global warming. // ⑧If we can't stop global warming, / the frequency of heavy downpours / may increase more and more. // ⑨Now / we must take more steps / to fight against global warming / and to protect the Earth. // (138 words)

🔊 意味のまとまりに注意して，本文全体を音読しよう！

New Words 新出単語の意味を調べよう			
animated 形 [ǽnɪmèɪtɪd] B1	1.	continuously 副 [kəntínjuəsli] B1	2.
annual 形 [ǽnju(ə)l] B1	3.	precipitation 名 [prɪsìpɪtéɪʃ(ə)n]	4.
barely 副 [béərli] B1	5.	abnormal 形 [æbnɔ́ːrm(ə)l] B1	6.
downpour 名 [dáʊnpɔ̀ːr]	7.	frequent 形 [fríːkwənt] B1	8.
rainfall 名 [réɪnfɔ̀ːl] B1	9.	frequency 名 [fríːkwənsi] B1	10.

A Comprehension
パラグラフの要点を整理しよう

Fill in the blanks in Japanese. 【思考力・判断力・表現力】

問題提起	映画『天気の子』のように，東京で2年以上も雨が降り続くような事態は実際に起こるだろうか。
考察	東京で2年以上も雨が降り続けるということは，現実には(1.　　　　　)。 ・東京の(2.　　　　　)はここ30年ほとんど変化していない。 ・しかし，地球温暖化を原因とした(3.　　　　　)が日本で頻発している。 ➡地球温暖化を止め，(4.　　　　　)を守る対策をとらなければならない。

B Key Sentences
重要文について理解しよう

Fill in the blanks and translate the following sentences.
【知識・技能】【思考力・判断力・表現力】

③ **It's unlikely that it would rain continuously for so long.**

◆It's unlikely that ... は「…はありそうもない」の意味で，Itはthat以下の内容を受ける形式主語。

◆2つ目のitは天候を表す文の主語。

訳: ....

④ **In fact, the annual precipitation of Tokyo has barely changed at all over the last thirty years.**

◆【事実と意見の区別】③の文で述べられた「意見」の根拠となる「事実」を述べた文である。(→ **Reading Skill**)

◆barelyは準否定語で，「ほとんど…ない」(= almost not) という意味。

訳: ....
....

⑤ **On the other hand, however, it is a fact that abnormal weather such as heavy downpours is becoming more frequent in Japan.**

◆【事実と意見の区別】it is a fact that ...「…は事実である，たしかに…である」という表現で，「事実」を表した文である。(→ **Reading Skill**)

訳: ....
....

⑨ **Now we must take more steps to fight against global warming and to protect the Earth.**

◆【事実と意見の区別】「〜しなければならない」という書き手の「意見」で，全体を締め括っている。

(→ **Reading Skill**)

◆andは 1.＿＿＿＿＿＿＿＿＿＿ ...とto protect ... という2つのto-不定詞を結びつけている。

訳: ....

No Rain, No Rainbow

Part 1

教科書 p.48-49

🔊 意味のまとまりに注意して，本文全体を聞こう！

1 ①The accident happened / in 2006, / when I was 18. // ②On my way home, / my motorcycle collided / with a car. // ③After a 12-hour-long surgery, / I barely survived. // ④However, / I was told / that I would spend the rest of my life / confined to bed. //

2 ⑤After six months / of physical rehabilitation, / I had learned to do many things / by myself / in a wheelchair. // ⑥Then, / I moved to another rehabilitation center, / where I met my mentor / in life. // ⑦He was undergoing rehabilitation / in the center, / too. // ⑧He always said to me, / "Opportunity is under your feet. // ⑨All you need to do / is recognize it." // ⑩He gave me several missions / to accomplish, / like going back home alone / on the train. // ⑪Completing the missions / he had given me, / I gradually gained confidence / in myself. // ⑫Finally, / leaving the rehabilitation center / in 2009, / I decided to live alone. // (140 words)

🔊 意味のまとまりに注意して，本文全体を音読しよう！

New Words 新出単語の意味を調べよう			
collide 動 [kəláɪd]	1.	surgery 名 [sə́ːrdʒ(ə)ri] B1	2.
confine 動 [kənfáɪn] B2	3.	physical 形 [fízɪk(ə)l] A2	4.
rehabilitation 名 [rìːəbìlɪtéɪʃ(ə)n]	5.	mentor 名 [méntɔːr] B2	6.
undergo 動 [ʌndərgóʊ] B1	7.	accomplish 動 [əká(ː)mplɪʃ] B1	8.
complete 動 [kəmplíːt] B1	9.		

 **Comprehension**
パラグラフの要点を整理しよう Fill in the blanks in Japanese. 【思考力・判断力・表現力】

三代達也さんの人生	
2006年	・(1.　　　)歳のときにバイクで事故にあう。 ➡大手術の末に一命をとりとめるが，寝たきりになると宣告される。
6か月間の リハビリ後	・車いすで多くのことが一人でできるようになる。 ・別のリハビリセンターに移り，人生の(2.　　　)に出会う。 ➡足元にある(3.　　　)に気づくことが大切だと言われる。
2009年	・リハビリセンターを退所し，（4.　　　）で暮らすことを決意する。

B Key Sentences
重要文について理解しよう Fill in the blanks and translate the following sentences.
【知識・技能】【思考力・判断力・表現力】

① **The accident happened in 2006, when I was 18.**

◆【パラグラフ間の関係 (時間的順序)】in 2006のような，時を表す表現に注意して出来事を整理すると話の流れが理解しやすくなる。(→ **Reading Skill**)

◆ whenは関係副詞(非制限用法)で，先行詞である2006に補足説明を加えている。

訳：_____

④ **However, I was told that I would spend the rest of my life confined to bed.**

◆ tell ＋ O1 ＋ O2 (＝ that-節)の受け身の文。that-節がwas toldの目的語になっている。

訳：_____

⑥ **Then, I moved to another rehabilitation center, where I met my mentor in life.**

◆ whereは関係副詞(非制限用法)で，先行詞であるanother rehabilitation centerに補足説明を加えている。

訳：_____

⑪ **Completing the missions he had given me, I gradually gained confidence in myself.**

◆ Completing ...は現在分詞の分詞構文。後に続く主節と自然につながるように意味を捉えるとよい。

◆ he had given meは直前のthe missionsを修飾している。heの前には関係代名詞のwhich [that]が省略されている。

訳：_____

■》 意味のまとまりに注意して，本文全体を聞こう！

3 ①In 2011, / I traveled to Hawaii alone. // ②It seemed like an enormous challenge, / but my friends gave me a push. // ③I enjoyed Hawaii / to the fullest, / which led to my next challenge: / a journey / around the world. //

4 ④I left Japan / in 2017 / and had fortunate encounters / during the journey. // ⑤Once, / my wheelchair got broken / on a stone pavement / in Florence, / Italy. // ⑥Then, / an Italian family / passing nearby / offered me help / and struggled to fix it / for me. // ⑦How lucky I was! //

5 ⑧I visited 23 countries / in nine months. // ⑨Through the journey, / I found / the world was still full of physical barriers. // ⑩At the same time, / I found / these barriers could be overcome / with the kindness of others. // ⑪The motorcycle accident was a "rain" / in my life, / but thanks to that rain, / I encountered many "rainbows" / — wonderful people / in the world. // (140 words)

■》 意味のまとまりに注意して，本文全体を音読しよう！

New Words 新出単語の意味を調べよう			
journey 名 [dʒə́ːrni] A2	1.	fortunate 形 [fɔ́ːrtʃ(ə)nət] B1	2.
pavement 名 [péɪvmənt] B2	3.	Florence [flɔ́ːr(ə)ns]	フィレンツェ
struggle 動 [strʌ́g(ə)l] B2	4.	barrier 名 [bǽriər] B2	5.
kindness 名 [káɪn(d)nəs] B1	6.		

A **Comprehension**
パラグラフの要点を整理しよう

Fill in the blanks in Japanese.

【思考力・判断力・表現力】

2011年	・友人に後押しされ，三代さんは一人でハワイ旅行に行く。
2017年	・(1.　　　　　　)の旅に挑戦する。 ・フィレンツェの石畳の上で車いすが壊れるが，イタリア人家族が車いすを (2.　　　　　　)しようとしてくれる。
世界一周後の気づき	
・物理的な障壁はたくさんあるが，それらは思いやりによって(3.　　　　　　)できる。	
・バイク事故は「雨」だったが，そのおかげで出会えたすばらしい人たちは「(4.　　　　　　)」だった。	

B **Key Sentences**
重要文について理解しよう

Fill in the blanks and translate the following sentences.

【知識・技能】【思考力・判断力・表現力】

③ I enjoyed Hawaii to the fullest, which led to my next challenge: a journey around the world.

◆【前の文全体を先行詞とする関係代名詞which】whichは非制限用法の関係代名詞で，ここでは前の文全体を先行詞とし，「そのことは…」と補足説明を加えている。(→ **Key Expression**)

◆ コロン以下でmy next challengeの具体的な内容が示されている。

訳 : _____

⑥ Then, an Italian family passing nearby offered me help and struggled to fix it for me.

◆ 前半部分はS＋V＋O₁＋O₂の構造になっている。andによって2つの動詞が等位接続されている。

◆ it = 1. _____

訳 : _____

⑩ At the same time, I found these barriers could be overcome with the kindness of others.

◆ these barriers = 2. _____ barriers

訳 : _____

⑪ The motorcycle accident was a "rain" in my life, but thanks to that rain, I encountered many "rainbows" — wonderful people in the world.

◆ ダッシュを用いて，直前の "rainbows" に補足説明を加えている。

訳 : _____

🔊 意味のまとまりに注意して，本文全体を聞こう！

Interviewer: ① I've heard / you're starting a new life / in Okinawa. // ② Could you tell me why? //

Tatsuya: ③ First of all, / I love Okinawa. // ④ I'm fascinated / by the amazing nature / and the kindness / of the people there. // ⑤ Also, / Okinawa gives high priority / to universal tourism, / which is accessible to all people / regardless of age, / nationality / and disability. // ⑥ There are things / I want to report on / as a wheelchair traveler. //

Interviewer: ⑦ I see. // ⑧ I'm looking forward to reading your report soon. //

Tatsuya: ⑨ Thank you. //

Interviewer: ⑩ You've challenged yourself / in many things / in your life / so far. // ⑪ What would you like to say / to those who are hesitating / to take a step forward / like you? //

Tatsuya: ⑫ Well, / I understand / you'll feel anxious / when you start something new. // ⑬ Just take it easy. // ⑭ People around you / are watching your efforts. // ⑮ They're ready / to help you. // (133 words)

🔊 意味のまとまりに注意して，本文全体を音読しよう！

New Words 新出単語の意味を調べよう			
fascinated 形 [fǽsɪnèɪtɪd] B2	1.	priority 名 [praɪɔ́ːrəti] B2	2.
universal 形 [jùːnɪvə́ːrs(ə)l] B2	3.	accessible 形 [əksésəb(ə)l] B1	4.
regardless 副 [rɪɡáːrdləs] B2	5.	disability 名 [dìsəbíləti] B1	6.

Fill in the blanks in Japanese.　　　　　【思考力・判断力・表現力】

三代達也さんへのインタビュー	
Q.	なぜ沖縄で新しい生活を始めようと思ったのか。
A.	・沖縄のすばらしい（1.　　　　　）や人々の優しさに魅了されたから。 ・沖縄はユニバーサルツーリズム（＝年齢，国籍，（2.　　　　　）の有無に関係なくだれもが利用しやすい旅行）を重視しているから。
Q.	一歩踏み出すことをためらっている人に伝えたいことは何か。
A.	・新しいことを始めるには（3.　　　　　）もあると思うが，周囲の人が助けてくれるので，（4.　　　　　）にやってほしい。

B Key Sentences
重要文について理解しよう

Fill in the blanks and translate the following sentences.

【知識・技能】【思考力・判断力・表現力】

④ **I'm fascinated by the amazing nature and the kindness of the people there.**

◆ the amazing natureとthe kindness of the people thereがandによって並列に結ばれている。

◆ there = in 1._____

訳：_____

⑤ **Also, Okinawa gives high priority to** |universal tourism|**, which is accessible to all people regardless of age, nationality and disability.**

◆ whichは非制限用法の関係代名詞で，先行詞のuniversal tourismに説明を加えている。

◆ regardless of ... は「…にかかわらず」という意味。

訳：_____

_____

⑪ **What would you like to say to those who are hesitating to take a step forward like you?**

◆ those who ... は「…する人」という意味。whoは主格の関係代名詞。

訳：_____

_____

⑮ **They're ready to help you.**

◆ They = 2._____

訳：_____

🔊 意味のまとまりに注意して，本文全体を聞こう！

1 ①In a village / in Bangladesh, / a man puts a spoonful of white powder / into a beaker / of dirty water / taken from a local pond. // ②He stirs it / and the water becomes clear / in a few minutes. // ③He then filters the water / and drinks it. // ④People say, / "That powder is magic!" //

2 ⑤The man's name / is Kanetoshi Oda. // ⑥In 1995, / he experienced the Great Hanshin-Awaji Earthquake. // ⑦At the time of that disaster, / tap water was cut off / and many people were in trouble. // ⑧He thought, / "How helpful it would be / if we could use muddy pond water / for drinking." //

3 ⑨The solution was unexpectedly close at hand. // ⑩He remembered / that the sticky component / in *natto* / — polyglutamic acid / — can purify water. // ⑪He spent years / experimenting in his lab / and finally succeeded / in developing water purifying powder / from polyglutamic acid. // (135 words)

🔊 意味のまとまりに注意して，本文全体を音読しよう！

New Words 新出単語の意味を調べよう			
Bangladesh [bæ̀ŋɡlədéʃ]	バングラデシュ	spoonful 名 [spúːnfùl]	1.
powder 名 [páudər] B1	2.	beaker 名 [bíːkər]	3.
stir 動 [stə́ːr] B1	4.	filter 動 [fíltər]	5.
tap 名 [tǽp] A2	6.	muddy 形 [mʌ́di] B2	7.
sticky 形 [stíki] B1	8.	polyglutamic 名 [pɑ̀(ː)liɡluːtǽmɪk]	9.
acid 名 [ǽsɪd] B2	10.	purify 動 [pjúərɪfàɪ] B1	11.
lab 名 [lǽb] B1	12.		

A Comprehension
パラグラフの要点を整理しよう

Fill in the blanks in Japanese.

【思考力・判断力・表現力】

問題提起：安全な水の確保
・阪神淡路大震災では(1.　　　　　)の供給が遮断され，多くの人々が困難を強いられた。
➡濁った池の水を(2.　　　　　)に利用できないか。
解決策：水質浄化剤の発明
・(3.　　　　　)のねばねば成分(＝ポリグルタミン酸)は，水を浄化する。
・小田兼利さんは，ポリグルタミン酸から水質浄化する(4.　　　　　)の開発に成功した。
➡スプーン1杯の白い粉が，濁った池の水を透明な水に変えた。

B Key Sentences
重要文について理解しよう

Fill in the blanks and translate the following sentences.

【知識・技能】【思考力・判断力・表現力】

① **In a village in Bangladesh, a man puts a spoonful of white powder into a beaker of** dirty water **taken from a local pond.**

◆ 過去の出来事であるが，生き生きと描写するために現在時制が用いられている。

◆ taken from a local pondは，後ろからdirty waterを修飾している。

訳：

⑧ **He thought, "How helpful it would be if we could use muddy pond water for drinking."**

◆ How helpful it would be if we could use …は仮定法過去。「もしも…を使うことができれば，どんなにか役立つだろうに」という意味。

訳：

⑨ **The solution was unexpectedly close at hand.**

◆ 【パラグラフ間の関係 (問題解決)】The solution was …から，このパラグラフでは第2パラグラフで提起された問題・課題への解決策が述べられていくとわかる。(→ **Reading Skill**)

訳：

⑪ **He spent years experimenting in his lab and finally succeeded in developing water purifying powder from polyglutamic acid.**

◆ spend＋時間＋〜ingは「〜して時間を過ごす」の意味。

訳：

教科書 p.60-61

🔊 意味のまとまりに注意して，本文全体を聞こう！

4 ①Unfortunately, / Oda's water purifier didn't sell well / in Japan. // ②However, / in 2004, / when the Sumatra-Andaman Earthquake occurred, / it was adopted / to help victims / in Thailand. // ③This attracted global attention / and it was subsequently used / in other countries / such as Mexico, / Bangladesh / and Somalia. //

5 ④Oda thought / just selling his product / was insufficient, / however. // ⑤So, / he taught the local people / how to effectively market it / in order to create sustainable businesses. // ⑥This has given them / both a steady supply of water / and new employment. // ⑦It has also improved their quality of life. //

6 ⑧Oda's water purifier is now sold / in over 40 countries / and provides safe drinkable water / to about 2.8 million people. // ⑨He says, / "Now I know / what I was born for. // ⑩While I am alive, / I wish to create a world / where everyone can get safe water." // (136 words)   🔊 意味のまとまりに注意して，本文全体を音読しよう！

New Words 新出単語の意味を調べよう			
purifier 名 [pjúərɪfàɪər]	1.	Sumatra [sumáːtrə]	スマトラ島
Andaman [ǽndəmən]	アンダマン諸島	adopt 動 [ədá(ː)pt] B1	2.
subsequently 副 [sʌ́bsɪkw(ə)ntli]	3.	Somalia [səmáːliə]	ソマリア
insufficient 形 [ìnsəfíʃ(ə)nt] B2	4.	effectively 副 [ɪféktɪvli] B2	5.
employment 名 [ɪmplɔ́ɪmənt] B1	6.	drinkable 形 [dríŋkəb(ə)l] B2	7.

A Comprehension
パラグラフの要点を整理しよう

Fill in the blanks in Japanese.　【思考力・判断力・表現力】

小田さんの発明した水質浄化剤		
過去	・スマトラ島沖地震の被災者を援助するため，（1.　　　　　）で採用された。	
	➡世界的な（2.　　　　　）を集め，他の国々でも使用されるようになった。	
小田さんの考えと取り組み：		
持続可能なビジネスを目指して，現地の人々に効果的な販売方法を教えた。		
➡安定した水の供給と新しい（3.　　　　　）を創出し，人々の生活の質を向上させた。		
現在	・（4.　　　　　）か国以上で販売され，約280万人が浄化された水を飲んでいる。	

B Key Sentences
重要文について理解しよう

Fill in the blanks and translate the following sentences.

【知識・技能】【思考力・判断力・表現力】

① **Unfortunately, Oda's water purifier didn't sell well in Japan.**

◆【文修飾副詞】副詞 unfortunately は「残念なことに」と文全体を修飾している。（→ **Key Expression**）

訳：

③ **This attracted global attention and it was subsequently used in other countries such as Mexico, Bangladesh and Somalia.**

◆ This は，スマトラ島沖地震の際にタイの被災者の支援に小田さんの水質浄化剤が使われたことを指す。

◆ it = 1.

訳：

⑤ **So, he taught the local people how to effectively market it in order to**
　　　　S　V　　　　O₁　　　　　　　O₂
create sustainable businesses.

◆ S＋V＋O₁＋O₂ の文。how to 〜 の to と動詞の原形の間に effectively という副詞が挿入されている。

◆ it = 2.

訳：

⑨ **He says, "Now I know what I was born for."**

◆ what ... for は「何を求めて…か，何のために…か」という意味。what I was born for は，「生まれてきた意味，人生の目的」くらいの意味。

訳：

教科書 p.64-65

🔊 意味のまとまりに注意して，本文全体を聞こう！

①In developing countries, / there are still many people / who cannot get safe drinking water. // ②Building water wells / might be one way / to help these people. // ③However, / there are some points / that need to be considered. //

④1. Just building water wells / is not enough. //

⑤Water wells sometimes stop being used / when the equipment gets broken. // ⑥In some cases, / equipment parts are stolen / to be sold / for profit. // ⑦It is important / to find ways / in which local people can use and manage the wells sustainably. // ⑧We need to have a long-term perspective. //

⑨2. Situations differ / from place to place. //

⑩Some places urgently need wells / to secure water, / while others need developed water supply systems / rather than wells. // ⑪We have to grasp the actual situations / and provide adequate support / that meets the needs / of each case. // (133 words)

🔊 意味のまとまりに注意して，本文全体を音読しよう！

New Words 新出単語の意味を調べよう			
equipment 名 [ɪkwípmənt] B1	1.	sustainably 副 [səstéɪnəb(ə)li]	2.
perspective 名 [pərspéktɪv] B2	3.	differ 動 [dífər] B1	4.
urgently 副 [ə́:rdʒ(ə)ntli] B2	5.	secure 動 [sɪkjúər]	6.
grasp 動 [grǽsp]	7.	adequate 形 [ǽdɪkwət] B2	8.

A Comprehension
パラグラフの要点を整理しよう

Fill in the blanks in Japanese.

【思考力・判断力・表現力】

発展途上国での井戸建設支援にあたって重要なこと
1）単に井戸を建設するだけでは（1.　　　　　　　）である。
…（2.　　　　　　　）が井戸を管理できるようにしなければならない。
2）（3.　　　　　　　）は場所によって異なる。
…水を確保するために，（4.　　　　　　　）が必要な場所もあれば，給水システムが必要な場所も 　あるので，現地の実状を把握して，そのニーズを満たす援助をしなければならない。

B Key Sentences
重要文について理解しよう

Fill in the blanks and translate the following sentences.

【知識・技能】【思考力・判断力・表現力】

⑤ **Water wells sometimes stop being used when the equipment gets broken.**

◆ stop ～ing「～することをやめる」の～ing が，being used という受動態になっている。

訳：＿＿＿＿＿＿＿＿＿＿＿＿＿＿＿＿＿＿＿＿＿

⑦ **It is important to find ways in which local people can use and manage the wells sustainably.**

◆ which の先行詞は 1.＿＿＿＿＿＿＿であり，前置詞 in ＋関係代名詞 which 以下が先行詞を修飾している。

訳：＿＿＿＿＿＿＿＿＿＿＿＿＿＿＿＿＿＿＿＿＿
＿＿＿＿＿＿＿＿＿＿＿＿＿＿＿＿＿＿＿＿＿

⑩ **Some places urgently need wells to secure water, while others need developed water supply systems rather than wells.**

◆ Some places …, while others（＝ other 2.＿＿＿＿＿＿＿）～は「…する場所もあれば，～する場所もある」の意味。while は「だが一方」という意味で，対照的なことがらを結びつける接続詞。

訳：＿＿＿＿＿＿＿＿＿＿＿＿＿＿＿＿＿＿＿＿＿
＿＿＿＿＿＿＿＿＿＿＿＿＿＿＿＿＿＿＿＿＿

⑪ **We have to grasp the actual situations and provide adequate support that meets the needs of each case.**

◆ have to ～は 2 つの動詞の原形 grasp と provide の両方にかかっている。

◆ that は主格の関係代名詞で，先行詞の adequate support を that 以下の節が修飾している。

訳：＿＿＿＿＿＿＿＿＿＿＿＿＿＿＿＿＿＿＿＿＿
＿＿＿＿＿＿＿＿＿＿＿＿＿＿＿＿＿＿＿＿＿

教科書 p.68-69

🔊 意味のまとまりに注意して，本文全体を聞こう！

1 ①Do you know this woman? // ②Maybe / you have seen her / on TV. // ③She is Sazae, / the main character / in *Sazae-san*. // ④*Sazae-san* is one of the most popular animated cartoons / and is loved / by people / of all ages. // ⑤It is based on the comic / with the same title / illustrated by Machiko Hasegawa. //

2 ⑥*Sazae-san* originally appeared / in a local newspaper / in Kyushu / as a series of four-frame comics / in 1946. // ⑦Each episode illustrates Sazae's daily life / with her family members, / friends / and neighbors. //

3 ⑧Sazae is a stay-at-home mom / with a two-year-old son / and lives / in her parents' home / with her three-generation family. // ⑨She is an energetic and active woman. // ⑩She is a little absent-minded / and sometimes makes a lot of mistakes, / but her cheerfulness makes people around her happy. // (127 words)

🔊 意味のまとまりに注意して，本文全体を音読しよう！

New Words 新出単語の意味を調べよう			
illustrate 動 [íləstrèɪt] B2	1.	frame 名 [fréɪm] A2	2.
episode 名 [épɪsòʊd] A2	3.	cheerfulness 名 [tʃíərf(ə)lnəs] B2	4.

A Comprehension
パラグラフの要点を整理しよう

Fill in the blanks in Japanese.

【思考力・判断力・表現力】

『サザエさん』	
主人公サザエ：専業主婦で，2歳の息子とともに(1.　　　　　)の家に3世代で暮らしている。元気で活発。うっかり者で(2.　　　　　)も多いが，明るく周囲を楽しませている。	
アニメ 『サザエさん』	・長谷川町子さんの漫画が原作で，あらゆる(3.　　　　　)の人に愛されている。
原作漫画 『サザエさん』	・九州の(4.　　　　　)に4コマ漫画として登場した。 ・サザエの家族や友人，近所の人々との日常生活が描かれている。

B Key Sentences
重要文について理解しよう

Fill in the blanks and translate the following sentences.

【知識・技能】【思考力・判断力・表現力】

④ *Sazae-san* is one of the most popular animated cartoons and is loved by people of all ages.

◆ andによって2つの動詞isとis lovedが並列に結ばれている。

訳：＿＿＿＿＿＿＿＿＿＿＿＿＿＿＿＿＿＿＿＿＿＿＿＿＿＿＿＿＿＿＿＿＿＿＿＿

⑤ It is based on the comic with the same title illustrated by Machiko Hasegawa.

◆ It = 1.＿＿＿＿＿＿＿＿

◆ 前置詞句と過去分詞の両方がthe comicを後置修飾している。

訳：＿＿＿＿＿＿＿＿＿＿＿＿＿＿＿＿＿＿＿＿＿＿＿＿＿＿＿＿＿＿＿＿＿＿＿＿

⑧ Sazae is a stay-at-home mom with a two-year-old son and lives in her parents' home with her three-generation family.

◆ withに導かれる前置詞句が2つあり，with a two-year-old sonはa stay-at-home momを，with her three-generation familyは2.＿＿＿＿＿＿＿＿を修飾している。

訳：＿＿＿＿＿＿＿＿＿＿＿＿＿＿＿＿＿＿＿＿＿＿＿＿＿＿＿＿＿＿＿＿＿＿＿＿
＿＿＿＿＿＿＿＿＿＿＿＿＿＿＿＿＿＿＿＿＿＿＿＿＿＿＿＿＿＿＿＿＿＿＿＿＿＿

⑩ She is a little absent-minded and sometimes makes a lot of mistakes, but her cheerfulness makes people around her happy.

◆【名詞構文】her cheerfulnessは，She is cheerful.という内容を名詞句にして表した名詞構文である。

(→ Key Expression)

訳：＿＿＿＿＿＿＿＿＿＿＿＿＿＿＿＿＿＿＿＿＿＿＿＿＿＿＿＿＿＿＿＿＿＿＿＿
＿＿＿＿＿＿＿＿＿＿＿＿＿＿＿＿＿＿＿＿＿＿＿＿＿＿＿＿＿＿＿＿＿＿＿＿＿＿

Sazae-san and Machiko Hasegawa   Part 2

教科書 p.70-71

🔊 意味のまとまりに注意して，本文全体を聞こう！

4 ①In the Showa era, / a "good wife and wise mother" / was the ideal image / of Japanese women. // ②It was thought / that women should be modest, / ladylike, / and faithful / to their husbands. //

5 ③On the other hand, / Sazae has an equal relationship / with her husband, / Masuo. // ④She is honest / and always expresses her opinions openly / and lives her own way. // ⑤This is a different image / from that of most Japanese women / at that time. //

6 ⑥Machiko Hasegawa once said, / "I want many people / to laugh every day." // ⑦She also said, / "If there is a woman / who is always cheerful and honest, / she can motivate those around her / to make the world brighter." // ⑧She hoped / many people would lead a happy life, / so she described Sazae / as her ideal image / of a cheerful and honest woman. //

(132 words)   🔊 意味のまとまりに注意して，本文全体を音読しよう！

New Words 新出単語の意味を調べよう			
wise 形 [wáɪz] A2	1.	modest 形 [mɑ́(:)dəst] B2	2.
ladylike 形 [léɪdilàɪk]	3.	faithful 形 [féɪθf(ə)l] B1	4.
relationship 名 [rɪléɪʃ(ə)nʃ ìp] B1	5.	openly 副 [óʊp(ə)nli] B2	6.

 **Comprehension**
パラグラフの要点を整理しよう

Fill in the blanks in Japanese. 【思考力・判断力・表現力】

昭和の女性像	⟷	サザエの人物像
・「(1.　　　　　)」が理想。 ・(2.　　　　　)で女性らしく，夫に忠実であるべき。		・夫のマスオと(3.　　　　　)な関係。 ・正直で，率直に意見を言い，自分らしく生きている。

長谷川町子さんの思い
・毎日たくさんの人に幸せに生きてほしい。 ➡彼女の(4.　　　　　)として，明るく正直な女性としてサザエを描いた。

B Key Sentences
重要文について理解しよう

Fill in the blanks and translate the following sentences.
【知識・技能】【思考力・判断力・表現力】

② **It was thought that women should be modest, ladylike, and faithful to their husbands.**

◆ Itは形式主語で，that以下の内容を指す。It is thought that ... で「…と考えられている」の意味。

訳：＿＿＿＿＿＿＿＿＿＿＿＿＿＿＿＿＿＿＿＿＿＿＿＿＿＿＿＿

③ **On the other hand, Sazae has an equal relationship with her husband, Masuo.**

◆【パラグラフ間の関係 (対比・対照)】on the other handは「一方で」という対比・対照を表すつなぎの語句。(→ **Reading Skill**)

訳：＿＿＿＿＿＿＿＿＿＿＿＿＿＿＿＿＿＿＿＿＿＿＿＿＿＿＿＿

⑤ **This is a different image from that of most Japanese women at that time.**

◆ that = the 1.＿＿＿＿＿＿

訳：＿＿＿＿＿＿＿＿＿＿＿＿＿＿＿＿＿＿＿＿＿＿＿＿＿＿＿＿

⑦ **She also said, "If there is a woman who is always cheerful and honest, she can motivate those around her to make the world brighter."**

◆ She = 2.＿＿＿＿＿＿＿＿＿＿＿＿＿＿ , she = a woman who is always cheerful and honest

◆ whoは主格の関係代名詞で，who以下の節が先行詞a womanを修飾している。

訳：＿＿＿＿＿＿＿＿＿＿＿＿＿＿＿＿＿＿＿＿＿＿＿＿＿＿＿＿

教科書 p.74-75

◀)) 意味のまとまりに注意して，本文全体を聞こう！

Machiko Hasegawa

1920	① She was born / in Saga. // ② She was a bright and tomboyish girl. // ③ She liked drawing pictures. //
1934	④ She became a private pupil / of manga artist / Suihou Tagawa. // ⑤ At the age of 15, / she made her debut / as a manga artist. //
1946	⑥ The local newspaper / in Kyushu / asked her / to contribute a series of four-frame comics. // ⑦ She hit upon an idea / that included the main characters / of *Sazae-san* / while walking / on a nearby beach. //
1947	⑧ She founded her own publishing company / with her sisters / in order to publish *Sazae-san* herself. //
1969	⑨ *Sazae-san* began / as a TV animation. //
1992	⑩ She passed away / at the age of 72 / and received the People's Honor Award / in the same year. //

⑪ Machiko was the first female professional cartoonist / in Japan. // ⑫ She was a strong and independent woman. // ⑬ Machiko, / as well as Sazae, / was an energetic and active woman / in the Showa era. // (141 words)

◀)) 意味のまとまりに注意して，本文全体を音読しよう！

New Words 新出単語の意味を調べよう

tomboyish 形 [tɑ́(:)mbɔ̀ɪʃ]	1.	pupil 名 [pjúːp(ə)l] B1	2.
debut 名 [déɪbjuː]	3.	upon 前 [əpɑ́(:)n] A2	4.
animation 名 [æ̀nɪméɪʃ(ə)n] B1	5.	cartoonist 名 [kɑːrtúːnɪst]	6.

A Comprehension　パラグラフの要点を整理しよう

Fill in the blanks in Japanese. 【思考力・判断力・表現力】

長谷川町子さんの人生	
1920年	佐賀県生まれ。明るく(1.　　　　　　　)な女の子だった。
1934年	田河水泡氏に弟子入りし，(2.　　　　　　　)歳で漫画家デビュー。
1946年	九州の新聞から4コマ漫画連載の依頼を受けた。
1947年	姉とともに(3.　　　　　　)を設立。
1969年	TVアニメ『サザエさん』が放送開始。
1992年	72歳で他界。同年，(4.　　　　　　)を受賞。

B Key Sentences　重要文について理解しよう

Fill in the blanks and translate the following sentences.

【知識・技能】【思考力・判断力・表現力】

⑤ At the age of 15, she made her debut as a manga artist.

◆ as は前置詞で「…として」という意味。

訳：

⑥ The local newspaper in Kyushu asked her to contribute a series of four-frame comics.

◆ ask ＋ O ＋ to ～は「Oに～するよう頼む」という意味。

訳：

⑬ Machiko, as well as Sazae, was an energetic and active woman in the

　　S　　　　　　　　　　　　　　V　　　C

Showa era.

◆ S ＋ V ＋ Cの文。energetic と active が等位接続されて woman を修飾している。

訳：

🔊 意味のまとまりに注意して，本文全体を聞こう！

1 ①Mago Nagasaka, / a street painter, / came across a photo / in 2016. // ②In the photo, / a child was standing / in a dump site overseas. // ③Shocked by the realities / of the world's waste, / in 2017 / he visited a slum / in Ghana / which was described / as the world's largest "graveyard" / for electronic devices. //

2 ④There, / young people were living desperately, / burning the electronic devices / to melt and extract the metals / inside them. // ⑤Those devices had been thrown away / by people / in developed countries / and then dumped / in Ghana. // ⑥Many of those young people / breathed in too much poisonous gas, / got cancer, / and died / in their thirties. // ⑦Mago was astonished / to know / that he was leading a comfortable life / at the expense of their lives. //

3 ⑧"I'm going to spread this fact / to developed countries / through the power of art," / said Mago. // ⑨So, / he started to create artworks / by using electronic waste (e-waste) / discarded in Ghana / and sold them. // (153 words)

🔊 意味のまとまりに注意して，本文全体を音読しよう！

New Words 新出単語の意味を調べよう			
dump 名 [dʌ́mp] B1	1.	slum 名 [slʌ́m]	2.
graveyard 名 [gréivjàːrd]	3.	extract 動 [ıkstrǽkt] B2	4.
metal 名 [mét(ə)l] A2	5.	poisonous 形 [póız(ə)nəs] B1	6.
astonished 形 [əstá(ː)nıʃt] B2	7.	discard 動 [dıskáːrd]	8.

 **Comprehension**
パラグラフの要点を整理しよう

Fill in the blanks in Japanese.

【思考力・判断力・表現力】

長坂真護さんのガーナとの出会い

- ・2016年，（1.　　　　　　　）に立つ子供の写真を見て，衝撃を受けた。
- ・2017年，ガーナにある世界最大の電子ごみの「（2.　　　　　　　）」を訪れた。

> ガーナの現実：若者たちは，電子機器を燃やして金属を抽出して生計を立てていて，多くの若者が（3.　　　　　　　）を吸い込み，がんになって30代で死んでいった。

- ・ガーナの惨状を伝えるため，（4.　　　　　　　）を使って作ったアート作品を制作，販売した。

B Key Sentences
重要文について理解しよう

Fill in the blanks and translate the following sentences.

【知識・技能】【思考力・判断力・表現力】

③ Shocked by the realities of the world's waste, in 2017 he visited a slum in Ghana which was described as the world's largest "graveyard" for electronic devices.

◆【分詞構文】Shocked …は過去分詞で始まる分詞構文。(→ **Key Expression**)
◆ whichは主格の関係代名詞で，which以下の節が先行詞a slum in Ghanaを修飾している。

訳 : _____

_____

_____

④ There, young people were living desperately, burning the electronic devices to melt and extract the metals inside them.

◆【分詞構文】burning …は現在分詞で始まる分詞構文。(→ **Key Expression**)

訳 : _____

_____

⑨ So, he started to create artworks by using electronic waste (e-waste) discarded in Ghana and sold them.

◆ 過去分詞で始まるdiscarded in Ghanaが，直前の名詞句electronic waste (e-waste)を後置修飾している。

訳 : _____

_____

🔊 意味のまとまりに注意して，本文全体を聞こう！

4 ①Mago believes / that sustainable economic growth is important. // ②So, / he has used the profits / from his artworks / to promote it / from the following perspectives: / education, culture and economy. //

5 ③In 2018, / Mago started the first school / in the slum, / "MAGO ART AND STUDY." // ④It will be free / to attend / as long as Mago lives. // ⑤Children learn subjects / like English and arithmetic / there. //

6 ⑥In August 2019, / Mago founded the "MAGO E-Waste Museum," / the first cultural facility / in the slums. // ⑦He believes / that the museum will help / to bring culture and new jobs, / and foster a hopeful new society. //

7 ⑧Mago has set his sights / on building a state-of-the-art recycling plant / in Ghana. // ⑨He is going to hire people / from the slums / to work / in his factory. // ⑩That way, / none of the local people / will need to do dangerous work / at the risk of their health. // ⑪Mago hopes / to turn the graveyard of e-waste / into a zero-pollution sustainable town. // (155 words)

🔊 意味のまとまりに注意して，本文全体を音読しよう！

New Words 新出単語の意味を調べよう			
economic 形 [ì:kəná(:)mɪk] B1	1.	growth 名 [gróʊθ] B1	2.
foster 動 [fá(:)stər]	3.	hopeful 形 [hóʊpf(ə)l] B1	4.
hire 動 [háɪər] B1	5.	none 代 [nʌn] B1	6.

 **Comprehension**
パラグラフの要点を整理しよう

Fill in the blanks in Japanese.　【思考力・判断力・表現力】

真護さんの考え：持続可能な(1.　　　　　　)成長が重要であり，教育・文化・経済の観点から促進したい。		
取り組み例	①教育面：(2.　　　　　　)で通える学校の設立	
	②文化面：(3.　　　　　　)施設の設立	
	③経済面：最新式の(4.　　　　　　)工場建設の計画	

B Key Sentences
重要文について理解しよう

Fill in the blanks and translate the following sentences.
【知識・技能】【思考力・判断力・表現力】

② So, he has used the profits from his artworks to promote it from the following perspectives: education, culture and economy.

◆ it ＝ 1.＿＿＿＿＿＿＿＿＿＿＿＿＿＿＿＿＿

◆【パラグラフ間の関係（例示）】education, culture and economyの3つの観点からどのような取り組みがなされたか，続く3つのパラグラフでそれぞれの具体例が示されている。(→ **Reading Skill**)

訳：

④ It will be free to attend as long as Mago lives.

◆ be free to ～は「～するのが無料である，無料で～できる」の意味。

◆ as long as …は「…する限り」という意味。

訳：

⑦ He believes that the museum will help to bring culture and new jobs, and foster a hopeful new society.

◆ 1つ目のandはcultureとnew jobsを，2つ目のandは2.＿＿＿＿＿＿＿＿…とfoster …をつないでいる。

訳：

⑩ That way, none of the local people will need to do dangerous work at the risk of their health.

◆ that wayは「そうすれば，そのようにして」という意味の表現。

◆ none of …は「…のうちのだれも～ない」という意味。

訳：

教科書 p.84-85

🔊 意味のまとまりに注意して，本文全体を聞こう！

Kumi: ① What do you think / about the e-waste problem? //

Takashi: ② New smartphones and tablets / are released / one after another. // ③ They look very attractive. // ④ But / we have to think twice / before buying a new device. // ⑤ We should ask ourselves / if we really need a new one. //

Kumi: ⑥ I agree with you, / Takashi. // ⑦ In addition, / once we've got a device, / we have to use it / until it no longer works. // ⑧ We have to treat it / with care. // ⑨ It's also important / to repair and reuse our devices. //

Vivian: ⑩ Exactly. // ⑪ We consumers should become more aware / of the e-waste problem. // ⑫ Also, / I think / the manufacturers should be responsible / for disposal of their products / when they are no longer usable. //

Takashi: ⑬ You have a good point! // ⑭ Governments should require the manufacturers / to collect e-waste / by setting up collection centers / or take-back systems, / either individually or collectively. //

Kumi: ⑮ Great. // (137 words)

🔊 意味のまとまりに注意して，本文全体を音読しよう！

New Words 新出単語の意味を調べよう

tablet 名 [tǽblət] B1	1.	manufacturer 名 [mæ̀njəfǽktʃ(ə)rər] B2	2.
disposal 名 [dɪspóuz(ə)l] B2	3.	usable 形 [júːzəb(ə)l]	4.
individually 副 [ìndɪvídʒu(ə)li]	5.	collectively 副 [kəléktɪvli]	6.

 **Comprehension**
パラグラフの要点を整理しよう

Fill in the blanks in Japanese.

【思考力・判断力・表現力】

電子ごみ問題に対する解決策		
消費者の役割	・新しい機器を買う必要が本当にあるのかどうか(1.　　　　　　　)。 ・機器が使えなくなるまで使う。 　┗━ 大切に使う，修理する，(2.　　　　　　　)する。	
メーカーの役割	・使えなくなった機器の(3.　　　　　　)まで責任を持つ。 ・収集センターや(4.　　　　　　)システムを設立する。	

B **Key Sentences**
重要文について理解しよう

Fill in the blanks and translate the following sentences.

【知識・技能】【思考力・判断力・表現力】

⑤ **We should ask ourselves if we really need a new one.**

◆ if ... は「…かどうか」の意味を表す接続詞で，whether ... と同じ意味を表す。

◆ a new one ＝ a new 1._____

訳: _____

⑦ **In addition, once we've got a device, we have to use it until it no longer works.**

◆ once ... は「いったん…すると」という意味の接続詞。

◆ no longer ... は「もはや…ない」の意味。

訳: _____

⑫ **Also, I think the manufacturers should be responsible for disposal of their products when they are no longer usable.**

◆ they ＝ their [the manufacturers'] 2._____

訳: _____

_____

⑭ **Governments should require the manufacturers to collect e-waste by setting up collection centers or take-back systems, either individually or collectively.**

◆ require ... to ～は「…に～するよう要求する」。

◆ either A or B で「AかBのどちらか，AまたはB」の意味。ここではAとBに副詞がきている。

訳: _____

_____

To Achieve Gender Equality

Part 1

教科書 p.88-89

🔊 意味のまとまりに注意して，本文全体を聞こう！

1 [1]Iceland is a Nordic island country / located in the North Atlantic Ocean, / with a population of about 350,000. // [2]The country has been ranked first / in gender equality / by the World Economic Forum / for over ten years. // [3]How are women playing an active role / in Icelandic society? //

2 [4]In Iceland, / more women are active / in politics / than in many other countries. // [5]About 40% / of the members / of parliament / are women. // [6]Women have a major influence / on policy making / regarding welfare, / education / and wages. //

3 [7]In addition, / the employment rate / of women in Iceland / is higher / than 80%. // [8]There is a good working environment / for women, / and many working mothers take their babies / to work / with them. // [9]The childcare leave system / is well developed, / and a high percentage / of men / as well as women / take childcare leave. // [10]Many companies are also trying / to eliminate the wage gap / between men and women. // [11]Iceland may be the best place / in the world / for working women / who have children. // (162 words)

🔊 意味のまとまりに注意して，本文全体を音読しよう！

New Words 新出単語の意味を調べよう			
Iceland [áɪslənd]	アイスランド	Nordic [nɔ́:rdɪk]	北欧の
Atlantic [ətlǽn(t)ɪk] B1	大西洋の	rank 動 [rǽŋk]	1.
gender 名 [dʒéndər] A2	2.	equality 名 [ɪkwá(:)ləti] B1	3.
forum 名 [fɔ́:rəm]	4.	Icelandic [aɪslǽndɪk]	アイスランドの

politics 名 [pá(:)lətìks] B1	5.	parliament 名 [pá:rləmənt] B2	6.
regarding 前 [rɪgáːrdɪŋ] B1	7.	wage 名 [wéɪdʒ] B2	8.
rate 名 [réɪt] A2	9.		

A Comprehension
パラグラフの要点を整理しよう

Fill in the blanks in Japanese.　　　【思考力・判断力・表現力】

アイスランド	
・北大西洋に位置する北欧の島国で，人口は約(1.　　　　　　)万人。 ・男女平等ランキングで10年以上1位となっている。	
女性の活躍	・(2.　　　　　　)の約40％が女性。 ・女性の就業率が80％を超えている。 ▶赤ちゃんを連れて出勤することができ，(3.　　　　　　)制度が充実している。 ▶多くの企業が男女間の(4.　　　　　　)をなくすように取り組んでいる。

B Key Sentences
重要文について理解しよう

Fill in the blanks and translate the following sentences.
【知識・技能】【思考力・判断力・表現力】

① Iceland is a Nordic island country located in the North Atlantic Ocean, with a population of about 350,000.

◆ 過去分詞1.　　　　　　と前置詞withが導く句がそれぞれa Nordic island countryを修飾している。

訳:

④ In Iceland, more women are active in politics than in many other countries.

◆【比較の対象の省略】than以下で表されている比較の対象は，省略を補うとthan (women are active in politics) in many other countriesとなる。(→ Key Expression)

訳:

⑨ The childcare leave system is well developed, and a high percentage of men as well as women take childcare leave.

◆ 前半の節はS＋V＋C，後半の節はS＋V＋Oの構造になっている。

訳:

🔊 意味のまとまりに注意して，本文全体を聞こう！

4 ① How has Iceland achieved gender equality? // ② In Iceland, / it used to be common / for women / to do housework and childcare / as full-time housewives. // ③ Even if they were working, / women's income was much lower / than men's. // ④ Women felt dissatisfied / with such a situation. //

5 ⑤ On October 24, / 1975, / about 90% / of adult females / in Iceland / went on strike / to protest against gender inequality / in their workplaces and families. // ⑥ On that day, / they boycotted all their work and housework, / and gathered together / in a square / in the capital city, / Reykjavik. // ⑦ The strike made the men realize / that they could not live a single day / without women. //

6 ⑧ As a result of the strike, / Icelandic society started to change. // ⑨ In 1980, / the first female president / was elected. // ⑩ Social institutions and laws / for gender equality / were developed. // ⑪ The working conditions / for women / also improved, / and the wage gap was gradually reduced. // ⑫ These movements / toward gender equality / succeeded in making Iceland what it is now. // (158 words)

🔊 意味のまとまりに注意して，本文全体を音読しよう！

New Words 新出単語の意味を調べよう			
housewife 名 [háʊswàɪf] B2	1.	income 名 [ínkʌm] B1	2.
dissatisfied 形 [dɪ(s)sǽtɪsfàɪd] B2	3.	strike 名 [stráɪk] A2	4.
protest 動 [prətést] B2	5.	inequality 名 [ìnɪkwá(:)ləti]	6.
boycott 動 [bɔ́ɪkà(:)t]	7.	Reykjavik [réɪkjəvìk]	レイキャビク
elect 動 [ɪlékt] B2	8.	institution 名 [ìnstɪtjú:ʃ(ə)n] B2	9.

Fill in the blanks in Japanese. 【思考力・判断力・表現力】

アイスランドでのストライキ発生	
ストライキ前	・多くの女性が(1.　　　　　　　)として家事や育児をするのが一般的だった。 ・女性の収入は男性よりはるかに低かった。
↓　1975年10月24日，男女平等を求めるストライキが発生。	
ストライキ後	・初の女性(2.　　　　　　　)が選出された。 ・男女平等のための社会制度と(3.　　　　　　　)が整備された。 ・女性の(4.　　　　　　)が改善され，男女の賃金格差が縮小した。

B Key Sentences
重要文について理解しよう

Fill in the blanks and translate the following sentences.
【知識・技能】【思考力・判断力・表現力】

② In Iceland, [it] used to be common for women to do housework and childcare as full-time housewives.

◆ it is ... for A to ～の構文で，isがused to beになった形。itは形式主語で，to以下の内容を指す。to以下の意味上の主語は1.＿＿＿＿＿＿＿である。

訳：＿＿＿＿＿＿＿＿＿＿＿＿＿＿＿＿＿＿＿＿＿

⑦ The strike made the men realize that they could not live a single day
　　　 S　　　 V　　　 O　　　 C
without women.

◆ make＋O＋C（＝原形不定詞）で「Oに～させる」という意味。that以下はrealizeの目的語。

訳：＿＿＿＿＿＿＿＿＿＿＿＿＿＿＿＿＿＿

⑧ As a result of the strike, Icelandic society started to change.

◆【パラグラフ間の関係（原因・結果）】結果を表すas a result of ...というつなぎの語句から，前のパラグラフの内容に対する「結果」がこれ以降で述べられることがわかる。（→ **Reading Skill**）

訳：＿＿＿＿＿＿＿＿＿＿＿＿＿＿＿＿＿

⑫ These movements toward gender equality succeeded in making Iceland what it is now.

◆ making以下はmake＋O＋Cの形になっている。
◆ what it is nowは「現在の姿，現在のあり方」の意味で，itは2.＿＿＿＿＿＿＿を指す。

訳：＿＿＿＿＿＿＿＿＿＿＿＿＿＿＿＿＿

教科書 p.94-95

🔊 意味のまとまりに注意して，本文全体を聞こう！

Japan 120th / in Global Gender Equality Ranking //

① Japan has one of the highest gender inequality rates / in the world. // ② In the World Economic Forum's Global Gender Equality Ranking / in 2021, / Japan's scorecard was 120 / out of 156 countries. // ③ This ranking was the lowest / of the G7 countries. // ④ On the other hand, / Nordic countries, / including Iceland, / were at the top of the list. //

⑤ Why does Japan have such a low ranking? // ⑥ In the Global Gender Equality Ranking, / gender disparity is quantified and evaluated / in four areas: / politics, / economics, / education / and health. // ⑦ The gender gap / in Japan / is particularly large, / especially in the political and economic fields. // ⑧ The involvement of women / in these fields / is an urgent issue. //

⑨ The Japanese government is trying / to encourage gender equality / but we are not succeeding / in achieving it. // ⑩ We should learn / from Nordic countries / and try to change deeply rooted social practices. // ⑪ We must have a clear goal / — to create a better working environment / for both women and men / — and make continuous efforts / to realize it / for ourselves. // (166 words)

🔊 意味のまとまりに注意して，本文全体を音読しよう！

New Words 新出単語の意味を調べよう

ranking 名 [rǽŋkɪŋ]	1.	Norway [nɔ́ːrwèɪ]	ノルウェー
Namibia [nəmíbiə]	ナミビア	Rwanda [ruɑ́ːndə]	ルワンダ
Lithuania [lìθjuémiə]	リトアニア	Ireland [áɪərlənd]	アイルランド
Switzerland [swítsərlənd]	スイス	scorecard 名 [skɔ́ːrkɑ̀ːrd]	2.
disparity 名 [dɪspǽrəti]	3.	quantify 動 [kwɑ́(ː)ntɪfàɪ]	4.

B2

evaluate 動 [ɪvǽljuèɪt] B2	5.	economics 名 [ì:kəná(:)mɪks] B1	6.
particularly 副 [pərtíkjələrli] B1	7.	political 形 [pəlítɪk(ə)l] A2	8.
involvement 名 [ɪnvá(:)lvmənt] B2	9.	urgent 形 [ə́:rdʒ(ə)nt] B1	10.
continuous 形 [kəntínjuəs] B1	11.		

A Comprehension
パラグラフの要点を整理しよう
Fill in the blanks in Japanese.　【思考力・判断力・表現力】

男女平等ランキングにおける日本の状況
・2021年のランキングでは，日本は156か国中120位。(1.　　　　　　　)諸国の中で最低。
・日本は(2.　　　　　　)と経済の分野で男女格差が大きい。
➡北欧諸国にならって，深く根付いた(3.　　　　　　)を変えなければならない。
➡男女両方にとってよりよい(4.　　　　　)を実現するために持続的な努力が必要。

B Key Sentences
重要文について理解しよう
Fill in the blanks and translate the following sentences.
【知識・技能】【思考力・判断力・表現力】

④ On the other hand, <u>Nordic countries</u>, including Iceland, <u>were</u> at the top
　　　　　　　　　　　　　S　　　　　　　　　　　　　　V
of the list.

　◆ SとVの間にincluding Icelandという挿入句が入っている。

訳 :

⑥ In the Global Gender Equality Ranking, gender disparity is quantified
and evaluated in four areas: politics, economics, education and health.

　◆ quantifiedとevaluatedをandが等位接続しており，isに続いていずれも受け身を表している。

　◆ コロン以下で，four areasの具体的な内容が列挙されている。

訳 :

⑨ The Japanese government is trying to encourage gender equality but we
are not succeeding in achieving it.

　◆ it = 1.

訳 :

🔊 意味のまとまりに注意して，本文全体を聞こう！

1 ①Imagine an ocean / without fish. // ②Imagine your meals / without any seafood. // ③This is the future / if we do not think seriously / and act soon. //

2 ④This is the message / which the film / titled *The End of the Line* / gives us. // ⑤The film is the world's first major documentary / to focus on the impact / of overfishing / on the world's oceans. // ⑥Scientists predict / that if we continue to fish / as we are doing now, / we will see the end / of most seafood / by 2048. //

3 ⑦The film highlights / how many well-known species / are likely to die out. // ⑧For example, / bluefin tuna are among them. // ⑨In Spain, / the catch of bluefin tuna / has exponentially decreased: / 5,000 million tons / in 1999, / 2,000 million tons / in 2000, / and 900 million tons / in 2005. // ⑩However, / they are still being caught excessively / because of the increasing demand / for sushi / in Western countries. // ⑪The film implies / that a world with no fish / will experience mass starvation. // (156 words)

🔊 意味のまとまりに注意して，本文全体を音読しよう！

New Words 新出単語の意味を調べよう

documentary 名 [dɑ̀(:)kjəmént(ə)ri] B1	1.	overfishing 名 [òuvərfíʃɪŋ]	2.
highlight 動 [háɪlàɪt] B1	3.	bluefin 名 [blúːfìn]	4. (bluefin tuna)
exponentially 副 [èkspənénʃ(ə)li]	5.	excessively 副 [ɪksésɪvli]	6.
imply 動 [ɪmpláɪ] B2	7.	mass 形 [mǽs] B1	8.
starvation 名 [stɑːrvéɪʃ(ə)n] B2	9.		

A **Comprehension** パラグラフの要点を整理しよう　Fill in the blanks in Japanese.　【思考力・判断力・表現力】

| 魚の（1.　　　　　）を続ける | → | 近い将来，海から魚が消え，食卓から魚介類が姿を消す | → | 世界は大規模な（2.　　　　　）を経験する |

例）スペインのクロマグロ漁
50億トン（1999年）から9億トン（2005年）に激減したが，西洋諸国における寿司の流行に伴ってクロマグロの（3.　　　　　）が高まり，乱獲は今も続いている。⇒（4.　　　　　　）の危機

B **Key Sentences** 重要文について理解しよう　Fill in the blanks and translate the following sentences.
【知識・技能】【思考力・判断力・表現力】

⑤ The film is the world's first major documentary to focus on the impact of overfishing on the world's oceans.

◆ the first … to 〜は「〜した初の…」の意味になる。to 〜は不定詞の形容詞用法。

訳：＿＿＿＿＿＿＿＿＿＿＿＿＿＿＿＿＿＿＿＿＿＿＿＿＿

＿＿＿＿＿＿＿＿＿＿＿＿＿＿＿＿＿＿＿＿＿＿＿＿＿

⑥ Scientists predict that if we continue to fish as we are doing now, we will see the end of most seafood by 2048.

◆ asは「…するように」という接続詞で，we are doing now ＝ we are 1.＿＿＿＿＿＿ nowである。

◆ byは「…までには」という期限・限界を表す用法の前置詞。

訳：＿＿＿＿＿＿＿＿＿＿＿＿＿＿＿＿＿＿＿＿＿＿＿＿＿

＿＿＿＿＿＿＿＿＿＿＿＿＿＿＿＿＿＿＿＿＿＿＿＿＿

⑧ For example, bluefin tuna are among them.

◆ be among …は「（…の間にいる→）…の一つである」（＝ one of …）という意味。

◆ themとは，絶滅しそうなよく知られた種のこと。

訳：＿＿＿＿＿＿＿＿＿＿＿＿＿＿＿＿＿＿＿＿＿＿＿＿＿

⑩ However, they are still being caught excessively because of the increasing demand for sushi in Western countries.

◆ they ＝ 2.＿＿＿＿＿＿＿＿＿＿＿

訳：＿＿＿＿＿＿＿＿＿＿＿＿＿＿＿＿＿＿＿＿＿＿＿＿＿

＿＿＿＿＿＿＿＿＿＿＿＿＿＿＿＿＿＿＿＿＿＿＿＿＿

🔊 意味のまとまりに注意して，本文全体を聞こう！

4 ①Fishing with modern technology / is one of the most destructive activities / on earth. // ②Trawling, / in particular, / is very harmful. // ③To understand / how harmful it actually is, / let's compare trawling / for fish / in the ocean / to carrying out the same practice / on land. // ④Imagine a huge net / sweeping across the plains / of Africa / and catching lions, / elephants / and rhinos. // ⑤It also pulls out every plant and tree. //

5 ⑥Such destructive activity / is carried out / every day / in every sea and ocean / across the world. // ⑦People, / however, / pay little attention / to what is happening / under the sea / because it is invisible. //

6 ⑧Technology in the fishing industry / has advanced. // ⑨Ironically, / however, / this has contributed to overfishing. // ⑩The Global Positioning System / and sonars / are used / in fish finders. // ⑪They can find the locations / of a shoal of fish underwater, / give information / about their quantity, / and even make three-dimensional images. // ⑫Fishing boats are now equipped / with improved engines, nets and lines. // (155 words)

🔊 意味のまとまりに注意して，本文全体を音読しよう！

New Words 新出単語の意味を調べよう			
destructive 形 [dɪstrʌ́ktɪv] B1	1.	trawling 名 [trɔ́ːlɪŋ]	2.
particular 名 [pərtíkjələr]	3.	sweep 動 [swíːp] B2	4.
plain 名 [pléɪn]	5.	rhino 名 [ráɪnoʊ]	6.
invisible 形 [ɪnvízəb(ə)l] B2	7.	ironically 副 [aɪ(ə)rá(ː)nɪk(ə)li] B2	8.
position 動 [pəzíʃ(ə)n]	9.	sonar 名 [sóʊnɑːr]	10.

finder 名 [fáɪndər]	11.		shoal 名 [ʃóʊl]	12.	
underwater 形 [ʌ̀ndərwɔ́ːtər] B2	13.		quantity 名 [kwá(ː)ntəti] B1	14.	
dimensional 形 [dəmén ʃ(ə)n(ə)l]	15.		equipped 形 [ɪkwípt]	16.	

A Comprehension
パラグラフの要点を整理しよう

Fill in the blanks in Japanese.　　　　　　　　　【思考力・判断力・表現力】

乱獲を助長する科学技術の進歩
(1.　　　　　　)漁…網を底引きしてさまざまな魚を一網打尽にする漁法。地球上で最も破壊的な活動の一つ。
科学技術の進歩：(2.　　　　　　)とソナーを利用した(3.　　　　　　) 改良型の(4.　　　　　　)や網，糸を搭載した漁船

B Key Sentences
重要文について理解しよう

Fill in the blanks and translate the following sentences.
　　　　　　　　　　　　　　　【知識・技能】【思考力・判断力・表現力】

④ **Imagine a huge net sweeping across the plains of Africa and catching lions, elephants and rhinos.**

◆ imagine ... ～ing で「…が～するのを想像する」の意味。a huge net が動名詞 sweeping と catching の意味上の主語になっている。

訳：_____

_____

⑦ **People, however, pay little attention to what is happening under the sea because it is invisible.**

◆ pay little attention to ... は「…にほとんど注意を払わない」。

訳：_____

_____

⑪ **They can find the locations of a shoal of fish underwater, give information about their quantity, and even make three-dimensional images.**

◆ and によって，3つの動詞 find と 1._____ と (even) 2._____ が並列されている。助動詞 can はそのいずれにもかかっている。

訳：_____

_____

🔊 意味のまとまりに注意して，本文全体を聞こう！

7 ①Who is responsible / for the situation? // ②Consumers buy endangered fish / without thinking about the impact / on the environment. // ③Politicians ignore the advice and warnings / from scientists. // ④Fishermen break quotas / and fish illegally. // ⑤The global fishing industry / is slow to react / to the disaster / so near at hand. //

8 ⑥The documentary / *The End of the Line* / shows simple and possible solutions / for this international problem. // ⑦Every country needs to control fishing / by reducing the number / of fishing boats / across the world. // ⑧We should protect large areas / of the ocean / as marine reserves. // ⑨Consumers should buy fish / only from certified sustainable fisheries. //

9 ⑩"Overfishing is one of the great environmental disasters," / said one of the film producers. // ⑪"I hope / the film will change our lifestyles / and what we eat." // ⑫Charles Clover, / the author of the book / which the film is based on, / says, / "We must act now / to protect the sea / from overfishing / in order to pass rich marine resources / to the next generation." // (160 words)

🔊 意味のまとまりに注意して，本文全体を音読しよう！

New Words 新出単語の意味を調べよう			
politician 名 [pə(:)lətíʃ(ə)n] B1	1.	ignore 動 [ɪɡnɔ́:r] B1	2.
quota 名 [kwóʊtə]	3.	react 動 [riǽkt] B1	4.
marine 形 [mərí:n] B1	5.	reserve 名 [rɪzə́:rv] B1	6.

certified 形 [sə́:rtɪfàɪd]	7.	fishery 名 [fíʃ(ə)ri]	8.
Charles Clover [tʃɑ́:rlz klóuvər]	チャールズ・クローバー	author 名 [ɔ́:θər]	9. A2

A Comprehension
パラグラフの要点を整理しよう

Fill in the blanks in Japanese.　　　　　　　　【思考力・判断力・表現力】

魚の乱獲の深刻化		
原因	・消費者：環境への影響を考えず，（1.　　　　　　　　）の危機にある魚を買っている。 ・政治家：科学者の助言や警告を無視している。 ・漁業者：（2.　　　　　　）量を超えたり，違法な漁をしている。	
解決策	・各国が（3.　　　　　　）の数を減らしたり，海洋保護区を設定するべき。 ・消費者は，（4.　　　　　　）と認定された漁場で捕れた魚だけを買うべき。	

B Key Sentences
重要文について理解しよう

Fill in the blanks and translate the following sentences.
【知識・技能】【思考力・判断力・表現力】

⑤ **The global fishing industry is slow to react to the disaster so near at hand.**

◆ so near at handは「（時間的に）すぐ近くにある，そんなにもさし迫っている」という意味。

訳：＿＿＿＿＿＿＿＿＿＿＿＿＿＿＿＿＿＿＿＿＿＿＿＿＿＿＿＿＿＿＿

⑨ **Consumers should buy fish only from certified sustainable fisheries.**

◆ 2つの形容詞certifiedとsustainableがfisheriesを修飾している。

訳：＿＿＿＿＿＿＿＿＿＿＿＿＿＿＿＿＿＿＿＿＿＿＿＿＿＿＿＿＿＿＿

⑫ **Charles Clover, the author of the book which the film is based on, says, "We must act now to protect the sea from overfishing in order to pass rich marine resources to the next generation."**

◆ S＋V＋Oの文であり，1.＿＿＿＿＿＿＿＿＿＿＿がS，2.＿＿＿＿＿＿＿がV，ダブルクォーテーションでくくられた部分がOになっている。

◆ Charles Cloverとthe author of the book which the film is based onは同格の関係。関係代名詞whichは，前置詞onの目的語の働きをしている。

訳：＿＿＿＿＿＿＿＿＿＿＿＿＿＿＿＿＿＿＿＿＿＿＿＿＿＿＿＿＿＿＿

＿＿＿＿＿＿＿＿＿＿＿＿＿＿＿＿＿＿＿＿＿＿＿＿＿＿＿＿＿＿＿＿＿

＿＿＿＿＿＿＿＿＿＿＿＿＿＿＿＿＿＿＿＿＿＿＿＿＿＿＿＿＿＿＿＿＿

🔊 意味のまとまりに注意して，本文全体を聞こう！

①Does the film affect / consumer attitudes and intentions? //

②A survey was conducted / before and after the film's premiere / in theaters. // ③Before watching the film, / 26% of these audiences indicated / that they did not believe overfishing / to be a serious problem. // ④What happened / to this group / after watching the film? // ⑤Eighty-five percent of them answered / that it was quite a big problem. //

⑥The audiences were also asked / about their buying habits / before the film / and their intended buying habits / after the film. // ⑦The percentage of the audiences / who had the intention / to buy only sustainable fish / almost doubled / from 43% / to 84%. //

⑧The impact was even more profound / on the group / who were not aware of the problems / of overfishing. // ⑨Only 17% of this group / bought sustainable fish / before watching the film. // ⑩However, / after watching, / 82% said / they would now try / to buy sustainable fish. // (144 words)

🔊 意味のまとまりに注意して，本文全体を音読しよう！

New Words 新出単語の意味を調べよう			
analysis 名 [ənǽləsɪs] B1	1.	intention 名 [ɪnténʃ(ə)n] B1	2.
conduct 動 [kəndʌ́kt] B2	3.	premiere 名 [prɪmíər]	4.
indicate 動 [índɪkèɪt] A2	5.	profound 形 [prəfáund]	6.

A Comprehension

Fill in the blanks in Japanese.

【思考力・判断力・表現力】

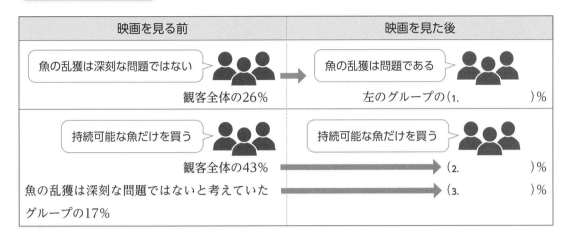

映画を見る前	映画を見た後
魚の乱獲は深刻な問題ではない 観客全体の26%	魚の乱獲は問題である 左のグループの(1.　　　　)%
持続可能な魚だけを買う 観客全体の43%	持続可能な魚だけを買う (2.　　　　)%
魚の乱獲は深刻な問題ではないと考えていた グループの17%	(3.　　　　)%

B Key Sentences

重要文について理解しよう

Fill in the blanks and translate the following sentences.

【知識・技能】【思考力・判断力・表現力】

③ Before watching the film, <u>26% of these audiences</u> <u>indicated</u> <u>that they did</u>

                                            S   V   O

not believe overfishing to be a serious problem.

◆ S＋V＋Oの文。that-節がindicatedの目的語になっている。

◆ believe＋O＋to ～は「Oが～すると信じる」という意味。

訳：

⑤ Eighty-five percent of them answered that it was quite a big problem.

◆ them＝this group＝26% of these audiences indicated that they did not believe overfishing to be
a serious problem

◆ it＝1.＿＿＿＿＿＿＿＿

訳：

⑧ The impact was even more profound on the group who were not aware

of the problems of overfishing.

◆ evenは「さらに」の意味で，比較級more profoundを強調している。

◆ whoは主格の関係代名詞で，who以下が先行詞のthe groupを修飾している。

訳：

Bats and Gloves Instead of Bombs and Guns Part 1

教科書 p.116-117

🔊 意味のまとまりに注意して，本文全体を聞こう！

1 ①In November 2006, / Mitsuru Okoso, / the leader of a Japanese NPO group, / received a letter / from his friend / Shoichi Ishida / in the U.S. // ②The letter said / a group of U.S. war veterans / wanted to play softball / against some Japanese veterans. // ③They had fought against Japan / in World War II. //

2 ④These veterans, / who were all 75 or older, / were members / of a world-renowned senior softball team / in Florida. // ⑤Ishida was a TV director / and had once made a documentary film / about the team. // ⑥One of the veterans told Ishida / about his wish / for the game, / and Ishida then asked Okoso / for his help. //

3 ⑦The man / who originated the idea / for the game / was Harvey Musser. // ⑧He had fought against Japan / on Leyte Island / during the war. // ⑨He got injured / in the left half of his body / and lost the sight / of his left eye / during the battle. // ⑩He said, / "We fought / in the war / but we do not hate the Japanese. // ⑪We want to fight with them again, / but this time, / through a softball game." // (174 words)

🔊 意味のまとまりに注意して，本文全体を音読しよう！

New Words 新出単語の意味を調べよう			
veteran 名 [vét(ə)r(ə)n] B2	1.	renowned 形 [rɪnáund]	2.
Florida [flɔ́ːrɪdə]	フロリダ	originate 動 [ərídʒənèɪt] B2	3.
Harvey Musser [háːrvi mʌ́sər]	ハーベイ・ムッサー	Leyte [léɪti]	レイテ（島）

A **Comprehension** パラグラフの要点を整理しよう　Fill in the blanks in Japanese.　【思考力・判断力・表現力】

元アメリカ軍兵士からの親善試合の依頼
・石田彰一さんが元アメリカ軍兵士たちのソフトボールチームの(1.　　　　　)映画を作成した。
・元兵士のハーベイ・ムッサーさんが石田さんに，日本の元兵士たちと(2.　　　　　)で対戦したいと依頼した。　　第二次世界大戦中，レイテ島の戦いで，左半身を負傷し，(3.　　　　　)の視力を失った。
・2006年11月，石田さんが大社充さんに依頼の(4.　　　　　)を出した。

B **Key Sentences** 重要文について理解しよう　Fill in the blanks and translate the following sentences.

【知識・技能】【思考力・判断力・表現力】

① In November 2006, Mitsuru Okoso, the leader of a Japanese NPO group,
［　＝　］

received a letter from his friend Shoichi Ishida in the U.S.
［　＝　］

◆ Mitsuru Okosoは the leader of a Japanese NPO groupと，his friendは Shoichi Ishidaと，それぞれ同格の関係になっている。

訳：_____

_____

③ They had fought against Japan in World War II.

◆ They = 1._____

◆ had foughtは過去完了形で，過去のある時点において，それより前に経験したことを表している。

訳：_____

⑥ One of the veterans told Ishida about his wish for the game, and Ishida then asked Okoso for his help.

◆ the veteransは（2.　　　　　）人の元兵士のこと。

訳：_____

_____

⑪ We want to fight with them again, but this time, through a softball game.

◆ them = the 3._____

訳：_____

🔊 意味のまとまりに注意して，本文全体を聞こう！

4 ① Okoso decided to help Ishida / and the veterans, / and started to look for Japanese senior players. // ② He needed at least 11 players, / but it was not an easy job / to find them. // ③ He set up a website, / made a leaflet, / and asked newspaper companies / and TV stations / to report this news. // ④ Soon / one player after another / responded to Okoso's plea. //

5 ⑤ One player had been a suicide attack diver. // ⑥ He was about to die / at the end of the war. // ⑦ Another had been a pilot / who had just barely escaped / from an attack / by American planes. // ⑧ Still another had experienced an aerial bombing / by a B29 / and lost many friends. // ⑨ All the players had gone through that terrible war, / but now wanted to enjoy a softball game / with Americans. //

6 ⑩ While gathering the members, / Okoso lost two of them / as they passed away / because of illness. // ⑪ It was a sad experience / for him / and the other members. // ⑫ However, / it strengthened his determination / to find a way / to successfully hold the game. // ⑬ Finally, / he was able to find 19 players. //

(177 words) 🔊 意味のまとまりに注意して，本文全体を音読しよう！

New Words 新出単語の意味を調べよう			
plea 名 [plíː]	1.	suicide 名 [súːɪsàɪd] B1	2.
diver 名 [dáɪvər] B1	3.	strengthen 動 [stréŋ(k)θ(ə)n] B1	4.
determination 名 [dɪtə̀ːrmɪnéɪʃ(ə)n] B1	5.		

 **Comprehension**
パラグラフの要点を整理しよう
Fill in the blanks in Japanese.　　　　　　　【思考力・判断力・表現力】

親善試合開催に向けた準備①（メンバー集め）
少なくとも（1.　　　　　）人の日本人選手が必要だったため，ウェブサイトとリーフレットを作り，新聞社や（2.　　　　　）にも告知を依頼した。
➡最終的に（3.　　　　　）名の選手を集めた。
・終戦時に戦死しそうになっていた水中特攻隊員 ・アメリカの戦闘機の攻撃から逃れたパイロット ・B29の（4.　　　　　）を経験して多くの友人を失った元兵士

B Key Sentences
重要文について理解しよう
Fill in the blanks and translate the following sentences.
【知識・技能】【思考力・判断力・表現力】

③ He set up a website, made a leaflet, and asked newspaper companies and TV stations to report this news.

◆ A, B, and Cの形で3つの動詞句（set up ... と 1.＿＿＿＿＿＿＿ ... と asked ...）が並列されている。

訳：＿＿＿＿＿＿＿＿＿＿＿＿＿＿＿＿＿＿＿＿＿＿＿＿＿＿＿＿＿＿＿

＿＿＿＿＿＿＿＿＿＿＿＿＿＿＿＿＿＿＿＿＿＿＿＿＿＿＿＿＿＿＿

④ Soon one player after another responded to Okoso's plea.

◆ S＋Vの文。Sは one player after another, Vは 2.＿＿＿＿＿＿ である。

訳：＿＿＿＿＿＿＿＿＿＿＿＿＿＿＿＿＿＿＿＿＿＿＿＿＿＿＿＿＿＿＿

⑦ Another had been a pilot who had just barely escaped from an attack by American planes.

◆ Another とは Another 3.＿＿＿＿＿＿ のこと。

◆ who は主格の関係代名詞で，who 以下の関係詞節が先行詞 a pilot を修飾している。

訳：＿＿＿＿＿＿＿＿＿＿＿＿＿＿＿＿＿＿＿＿＿＿＿＿＿＿＿＿＿＿＿

＿＿＿＿＿＿＿＿＿＿＿＿＿＿＿＿＿＿＿＿＿＿＿＿＿＿＿＿＿＿＿

⑩ While gathering the members, Okoso lost two of them as they passed away because of illness.

◆ while ～ing で「～している間に」という意味。主節の主語＋be-動詞が省略されていると考えるとよい。

◆ as は「…なので」という原因・理由を表す接続詞。

訳：＿＿＿＿＿＿＿＿＿＿＿＿＿＿＿＿＿＿＿＿＿＿＿＿＿＿＿＿＿＿＿

＿＿＿＿＿＿＿＿＿＿＿＿＿＿＿＿＿＿＿＿＿＿＿＿＿＿＿＿＿＿＿

教科書 p.120-121

🔊 意味のまとまりに注意して，本文全体を聞こう！

7 ①There were also other tasks / for Okoso / to do. // ②One was to find a stadium. // ③The location / of the game / was decided to be in Hawaii / as it is warm / and conveniently located / right between Japan and Florida. // ④Also, / it was the place / where the attack on Pearl Harbor occurred. // ⑤Okoso had difficulty booking a stadium, / but finally found one. //

8 ⑥Another task was to decide the date. // ⑦November or December / was thought to be the best, / as the playing seasons / for both sides / overlapped / during that time. // ⑧Some U.S. veterans suggested / the game be on December 7, / when they had experienced the attack on Pearl Harbor / in the U.S. time. // ⑨However, / the dates became December 18 and 19 / in 2007, / when the stadium was available. //

9 ⑩As the game was approaching, / Okoso found out / some of the U.S. members / had canceled their participation. // ⑪One said / he didn't feel like playing / with Japanese veterans / near Pearl Harbor. // ⑫Okoso realized / that there were still some people / in the U.S. / who saw the Japanese / as villains. // (172 words)

🔊 意味のまとまりに注意して，本文全体を音読しよう！

New Words 新出単語の意味を調べよう			
pearl 名 [pə́ːrl] B2	1.	harbor 名 [hɑ́ːrbər] B1	2.
overlap 動 [òuvərlǽp]	3.	suggest 動 [sə(g)dʒést] A2	4.
cancel 動 [kǽns(ə)l] B1	5.	villain 名 [vílən]	6.

Fill in the blanks in Japanese.

【思考力・判断力・表現力】

親善試合開催に向けた準備②（開催地・日程の調整）		
開催地	(1.　　　　　) ←	気候が(2.　　　　　)で，日米の中間にあり，かつて真珠湾攻撃があった場所。
日程	2007年 12月18・19日 ←	双方のシーズンが重なる11 ～ 12月で，(3.　　　　　)が利用可能だった日。
アメリカ側の選手の中には参加を(4.　　　　　)した人もいた。		

B Key Sentences
重要文について理解しよう

Fill in the blanks and translate the following sentences.

【知識・技能】【思考力・判断力・表現力】

④ **Also, it was the place where the attack on Pearl Harbor occurred.**

◆ where は関係副詞で，where 以下の関係詞節が先行詞 the place を修飾している。

訳：＿＿＿＿＿＿＿＿＿＿＿＿＿＿＿＿＿＿＿＿＿＿＿＿＿＿＿＿＿＿＿＿

⑤ **Okoso had difficulty booking a stadium, but finally found one.**

◆ book はここでは「…を予約する」という意味の動詞。

◆ one ＝ a 1.＿＿＿＿＿＿＿＿＿＿

訳：＿＿＿＿＿＿＿＿＿＿＿＿＿＿＿＿＿＿＿＿＿＿＿＿＿＿＿＿＿＿＿＿

⑦ **November or December was thought to be the best, as the playing seasons for both sides overlapped during that time.**

◆ November or December was thought to be the best. ＝ 2.＿＿＿＿＿＿＿＿ was thought 3.＿＿＿＿＿＿＿＿ November or December was the best.

◆ as は「…なので」という原因・理由を表す接続詞。

訳：＿＿＿＿＿＿＿＿＿＿＿＿＿＿＿＿＿＿＿＿＿＿＿＿＿＿＿＿＿＿＿＿

＿＿＿＿＿＿＿＿＿＿＿＿＿＿＿＿＿＿＿＿＿＿＿＿＿＿＿＿＿＿＿＿＿＿

⑩ **As the game was approaching, Okoso found out some of the U.S. members had canceled their participation.**

◆ as は「…するとき」という時を表す接続詞。

◆ 主節は find out (that) ＋ S ＋ V の構造になっている。

訳：＿＿＿＿＿＿＿＿＿＿＿＿＿＿＿＿＿＿＿＿＿＿＿＿＿＿＿＿＿＿＿＿

＿＿＿＿＿＿＿＿＿＿＿＿＿＿＿＿＿＿＿＿＿＿＿＿＿＿＿＿＿＿＿＿＿＿

Bats and Gloves Instead of Bombs and Guns Part 4

教科書 p.122-123

🔊 意味のまとまりに注意して，本文全体を聞こう！

①Play for Goodwill / — American and Japanese veterans / make runs, / not war / in Waipahu. //

②MORE THAN 60 years / after WWII, / veterans from the US and Japan / changed the battlefield / into the softball field. // ③Both teams / — 14 players / from Florida / and 19 / from Japan / — healed old wounds / by playing softball together. //

④The game was held / on December 19 / in Waipahu, / Hawaii. // ⑤It started / with 5 runs / by the US team / in the 1st inning / of the seven-inning game. // ⑥Though the Japanese fought back / in the 4th and 5th innings, / the US led the game / till the end. // ⑦The US won / with a final score of 14–2.

⑧After the game, / Mr. Yasukura, / an 84-year-old Japanese veteran, / laughed and said, / "We lost completely, / but I enjoyed the game. // ⑨I'm happy." // ⑩Mr. Devine, / an 82-year-old US veteran, / said, / "I couldn't think of a better way / for people / from two countries / to patch up old wounds / than to play softball together." // ⑪Players on both teams / used the game / to put the past behind / and build an unforgettable friendship. //

(172 words) 🔊 意味のまとまりに注意して，本文全体を音読しよう！

New Words 新出単語の意味を調べよう			
goodwill 名 [gùdwíl] B2	1.	Waipahu [waɪpáːhuː]	ワイパフ
battlefield 名 [bǽt(ə)lfiːld] B2	2.	heal 動 [híːl] B1	3.
wound 名 [wúːnd] B1	4.	inning 名 [ínɪŋ]	5.
Devine [dəváɪn]	ディバイン	patch 動 [pǽtʃ]	6.

 **Comprehension**
パラグラフの要点を整理しよう

Fill in the blanks in Japanese.

【思考力・判断力・表現力】

親善試合の様子		
参加人数	アメリカチーム(1.)名，日本チーム19名	
開催日	2007年12月19日	
試合経過・結果	・初回にアメリカが(2.)点先取。日本も4回と5回に反撃するが，終始アメリカが優勢で，14対2で勝利した。	

保倉さん（84歳）──（3. ）だったが，楽しかった。

ディバインさん（82歳）──ソフトボールは二国間の(4.)を癒やすのに最高の方法だった。

B Key Sentences
重要文について理解しよう

Fill in the blanks and translate the following sentences.

【知識・技能】【思考力・判断力・表現力】

⑥ Though the Japanese fought back in the 4th and 5th innings, the US led the game till the end.

◆ though は譲歩の副詞節を導く接続詞で，「…だが」という意味。

訳：

⑩ Mr. Devine, an 82-year-old US veteran, said, "I couldn't think of a better way for people from two countries to patch up old wounds than to play softball together."

◆ Mr. Devine と an 82-year-old US veteran は同格の関係。

◆ to patch up old wounds は不定詞の形容詞用法で，a better way を修飾している。

訳：

⑪ Players on both teams used the game to put the past behind and build an unforgettable friendship.

◆ S＋V＋O の文。to 以下は不定詞の副詞用法。to は put と build の両方にかかっている。

訳：

"Brighten the World in Your Corner" **Part 1**

教科書 p.132-133

🔊 意味のまとまりに注意して，本文全体を聞こう！

1 ①On December 4, / 2019, / the shocking news / of Dr. Tetsu Nakamura's death / traveled around the world. // ②Nakamura was shot dead / in a gun attack / while he was heading / for an irrigation canal project site. // ③Why was the famed Japanese doctor heading / for the irrigation canal site, / not a hospital? //

2 ④In 1984, / Nakamura was sent to Peshawar, / Pakistan / as a physician. // ⑤Once Nakamura started / performing his medical treatment, / he realized / how limited medical resources were. // ⑥There were only 16 sickbeds / for 2,400 patients. // ⑦Essential medical instruments / like stethoscopes / were totally lacking. // ⑧He even carried his patients / on his back / because there were no stretchers / in the hospital. //

3 ⑨By 1994, / Nakamura had established three clinics / in Afghanistan / to expand his treatment capacity. // ⑩In 2000, / a catastrophic drought struck Afghanistan, / leaving four million people / on the verge of starvation. // ⑪An increasing number of mothers / with dying children / visited Nakamura's clinics, / only to see their children lose their lives / while waiting in line. // ⑫Nakamura cried out / to himself, / "If there were an adequate supply / of food and water, / these children could survive!" // (178 words)

🔊 意味のまとまりに注意して，本文全体を音読しよう！

New Words 新出単語の意味を調べよう			
gun 名 [gʌ́n] A2	1.	irrigation 名 [ìrɪgéɪʃ(ə)n]	2.
canal 名 [kənǽl] B1	3.	famed 形 [féɪmd]	4.
Peshawar [pəʃɑ́:wər]	ペシャワール	Pakistan [pǽkɪstæn]	パキスタン
sickbed 名 [síkbèd]	5.	stethoscope 名 [stéθəskòup]	6.

totally 副 [tóut(ə)li] B1	7.	lack 動 [lǽk] B2	8.
stretcher 名 [strétʃər]	9.	expand 動 [ıkspǽnd] B1	10.
capacity 名 [kəpǽsəti] B1	11.	catastrophic 形 [kæ̀təstrá(:)fik] B2	12.
verge 名 [və́:rdʒ]	13.		

Ⓐ Comprehension
パラグラフの要点を整理しよう
Fill in the blanks in Japanese.　【思考力・判断力・表現力】

中村哲医師の人生	
1984年	パキスタンのペシャワールに派遣され，（1.　　　　　　　）として働き始めた。
1994年	アフガニスタンに3つの診療所を完成させた。
2000年	壊滅的な（2.　　　　　）がアフガニスタンを襲った。
	⇒十分な食料と（3.　　　　　　　）の必要性に気づいた。
2019年	（4.　　　　　　）の建設現場に向かう途中で射殺された。

Ⓑ Key Sentences
重要文について理解しよう
Fill in the blanks and translate the following sentences.
【知識・技能】【思考力・判断力・表現力】

⑩ In 2000, a catastrophic drought struck Afghanistan, leaving four million people on the verge of starvation.

◆ leaving ...は分詞構文で，a catastrophic drought struck Afghanistan, and left ...と考えるとよい。

◆ leave ... on the verge of starvationは「...を餓死寸前の状態にする」の意味。

訳：

⑪ An increasing number of mothers with dying children visited
　　　　　　　　　　　　　　　　S　　　　　　　　　　　　　　V
Nakamura's clinics, only to see their children lose their lives while
　　　　　　　　O
waiting in line.

◆ 主語の長いS＋V＋Oの文になっている。

◆ ..., only to ～は「...したが（残念なことに）～した」という期待はずれに終わった結果を表す。

◆ see＋O＋C（＝動詞の原形）は「OがCするのを見る」の意味。

訳：

🔊 意味のまとまりに注意して，本文全体を聞こう！

4 ①Afghanistan was once a rich agricultural country. // ②However, / years of drought / as well as continual foreign invasion / changed everything. // ③Many villagers could no longer continue farming / and had to abandon their villages. // ④Nakamura believed / the country would never be reconstructed / without the revival / of the abandoned farmland. //

5 ⑤Nakamura and his staff members / started to restore dried-up wells / and dig new wells. // ⑥It was impossible / to dig deeper into the wells / with human hands / because of a layer / of very large rocks. // ⑦Therefore, / they scraped out explosive materials / from unexploded bombs / and used them / to blow up the rocks. // ⑧Thanks to their devoted work, / the total number of wells / had reached 1,600 / by 2006. //

6 ⑨Nakamura and his members / launched the "Green Ground Project." // ⑩The main part of the project / was the construction / of a 25-kilometer-long irrigation canal / named "Aab-e-Marwarid." //

7 ⑪Nakamura had to learn the basics / of canal construction. // ⑫He walked around / looking at irrigation facilities / not only in Afghanistan / but also in Japan. // ⑬After seven years of hardship, / the canal finally reached its ultimate destination, / the Gamberi Desert. // (177 words)

🔊 意味のまとまりに注意して，本文全体を音読しよう！

New Words 新出単語の意味を調べよう			
continual 形 [kəntínju(ə)l] B1	1.	abandon 動 [əbǽnd(ə)n] B1	2.
reconstruct 動 [rì:kənstrʌ́kt]	3.	revival 名 [rɪváɪv(ə)l] B2	4.
dried 形 [dráɪd]	5.	impossible 形 [ɪmpá(:)səb(ə)l] A2	6.
layer 名 [léɪər] B1	7.	therefore 副 [ðéərfɔ̀:r] A2	8.

scrape 動 [skréɪp]	9.	explosive 形 [ɪksplóʊsɪv] B2	10.
launch 動 [lɔ́ːn(t)ʃ] B1	11.	Aab-e-Marwarid [à(:)bəmɑ(:)rwǽrɪd]	アーベ・マルワリード
ultimate 形 [ʌ́ltɪmət] B2	12.	destination 名 [dèstɪnéɪʃ(ə)n] B1	13.
Gamberi [ɡǽmbəri]	ガンベリ	desert 名 [dézərt] A2	14.

A Comprehension
パラグラフの要点を整理しよう

Fill in the blanks in Japanese.　【思考力・判断力・表現力】

アフガニスタンの状況	
・外国の(1.　　　　　　)と何年も続く干ばつによって，農地は荒廃した。	
・復興には，放棄された(2.　　　　　　)の再生が必須。	
中村さんらの取り組み	①枯れた井戸の修復と新しい井戸の(3.　　　　　　)
	②全長25キロの(4.　　　　　　)の建設

B Key Sentences
重要文について理解しよう

Fill in the blanks and translate the following sentences.
【知識・技能】【思考力・判断力・表現力】

④ Nakamura believed the country would never be reconstructed without the revival of the abandoned farmland.

◆ the country ＝ 1.＿＿＿＿＿＿＿＿＿＿＿＿＿＿

◆ would never ～ without … は「…なしにはけっして～しないだろう」という意味。

訳：＿＿＿＿＿＿＿＿＿＿＿＿＿＿＿＿＿＿＿＿＿＿＿＿＿＿＿＿＿＿＿

⑦ Therefore, they scraped out explosive materials from unexploded bombs and used them to blow up the rocks.

◆ they ＝ Nakamura and his staff members,　them ＝ 2.＿＿＿＿＿＿＿＿＿＿

訳：＿＿＿＿＿＿＿＿＿＿＿＿＿＿＿＿＿＿＿＿＿＿＿＿＿＿＿＿＿＿＿

⑫ He walked around looking at irrigation facilities not only in Afghanistan but also in Japan.

◆ looking … は「～しながら」という付帯状況を表す分詞構文。

訳：＿＿＿＿＿＿＿＿＿＿＿＿＿＿＿＿＿＿＿＿＿＿＿＿＿＿＿＿＿＿＿

🔊 意味のまとまりに注意して，本文全体を聞こう！

8 ①In 2003, / Nakamura received the Ramon Magsaysay Award, / which is regarded / as the Asian version / of the Nobel Prize. // ②In addition, / in 2019, / he was granted honorary citizenship / by the Afghan government / for his decades of humanitarian work / in the country. // ③In the same year, / however, / his tragic incident happened. // ④Many people / in the world / mourned his sudden death. // ⑤Many Afghans / living in Japan / gathered / to show their deep grief. //

9 ⑥Peshawar-kai is an organization / which has supported Nakamura's work / physically and spiritually. // ⑦It was established / in 1983 / to back up his work / in Pakistan. // ⑧After Nakamura's death, / it declared / it would continue all the work / he had undertaken. // ⑨The local staff regard themselves / as the students / of the Nakamura school / and share his philosophy, / "Brighten the world / in your corner." //

10 ⑩In the Gamberi Desert, / which was once feared / as the desert of death, / we can now see trees growing thickly. // ⑪We can also hear songbirds chirping / and frogs croaking. // ⑫The Aab-e-Marwarid Canal / supports the livelihoods / of 600,000 farmers / in the area / along the canal / today. //

(175 words) 🔊 意味のまとまりに注意して，本文全体を音読しよう！

New Words 新出単語の意味を調べよう			
Ramon Magsaysay [rɑ(:)mɔ́:n mɑ(:)gsáɪsaɪ]	ラモン・マグサイサイ	regard 動 [rɪgáːrd] B1	1.
honorary 形 [á(:)nərèri]	2.	citizenship 名 [sítɪz(ə)nʃìp] B1	3.
Afghan [ǽfgæn]	アフガニスタンの	humanitarian 形 [hjumǽnɪtéəriən]	4.
tragic 形 [trǽdʒɪk] B1	5.	incident 名 [ínsɪd(ə)nt] B1	6.

mourn 動 [mɔ́:rn] B1	7.	grief 名 [grí:f] B2	8.
spiritually 副 [spírɪtʃu(ə)li]	9.	undertake 動 [ʌ̀ndərtéɪk] B2	10.
philosophy 名 [fəlá(:)səfi] B1	11.	brighten 動 [bráɪt(ə)n]	12.
thickly 副 [θíkli] B2	13.	songbird 名 [sɔ́:ŋbə̀:rd]	14.
chirp 動 [tʃə́:rp]	15.	croak 動 [króuk]	16.
livelihood 名 [láɪvlihùd]	17.		

A Comprehension パラグラフの要点を整理しよう　Fill in the blanks in Japanese.　【思考力・判断力・表現力】

中村医師の功績	
2003年	ラモン・マグサイサイ賞を受賞した。
2019年	アフガニスタンの(1.　　　　　)を授与された。

死後も引き継がれていく中村医師の遺志：

・中村医師の活動を支えてきたペシャワール会が，彼の(2.　　　　　)を引き継ぐと宣言した。

・ガンベリ(3.　　　　　)には緑がよみがえった。

・マルワリード用水路は周辺の農民の(4.　　　　　)を支えている。

B Key Sentences 重要文について理解しよう　Fill in the blanks and translate the following sentences.
【知識・技能】【思考力・判断力・表現力】

② In addition, in 2019, he was granted honorary citizenship by the Afghan government for his decades of humanitarian work in the country.

◆ he was granted honorary citizenship by the Afghan governmentは, the Afghan government granted him honorary citizenship (S＋V＋O₁＋O₂の文)の受動態である。

訳：

⑩ In the Gamberi Desert, which was once feared as the desert of death, we can now see trees growing thickly.

◆ whichは非制限用法の関係代名詞で，関係詞節はthe Gamberi Desertに追加説明を加えている。

◆ see＋O＋C (＝現在分詞)は「OがCしているのを見る」という意味。

訳：

"Brighten the World in Your Corner"

Part 4

教科書 p.140-141

🔊 意味のまとまりに注意して，本文全体を聞こう！

Interviewer: ① Could you tell us / about your new song / "A grain of wheat — Moment—"? //

Sada: ② Yes. // ③ I wrote this song / to dedicate to Tetsu Nakamura. // ④ Many Afghans were suffering / from bitter civil wars / and devastating droughts. // ⑤ Nakamura worked there / as a physician / for over thirty years / and maintained / merely offering medical services / was insufficient. //

Interviewer: ⑥ What do you mean / by "insufficient"? //

Sada: ⑦ Well. // ⑧ Nakamura believed / adequate food and water supplies / should come before medical care. // ⑨ So, / he constructed an irrigation canal / under the slogan, / "One canal / instead of 100 clinics." //

Interviewer: ⑩ I see. // ⑪ Have you met Dr. Nakamura before? //

Sada: ⑫ Unfortunately, / no. // ⑬ Since I knew some members of Peshawar-kai, / I had expected / I would see him someday. // ⑭ So / I was really shocked / to hear / that a humanitarian like him / was shot dead / by an armed group. // ⑮ Though I couldn't have a chance / to talk with him directly, / I feel / as if he had helped me make this song. // ⑯ I strongly believe / the seeds / he sowed / in Afghanistan / will continue to grow. // ⑰ We will never forget his kind smile / and noble soul. // (175 words)

🔊 意味のまとまりに注意して，本文全体を音読しよう！

New Words 新出単語の意味を調べよう			
grain 名 [gréin] B2	1.	dedicate 動 [dédɪkèɪt] B1	2.
civil 形 [sív(ə)l] B1	3.	merely 副 [míərli] B1	4.

construct 動 [kənstrʌ́kt] B1	5.	directly 副 [dəréktli] B1	6.
noble 形 [nóub(ə)l] B2	7.	soul 名 [sóul] B1	8.

A Comprehension
パラグラフの要点を整理しよう

Fill in the blanks in Japanese.　　　【思考力・判断力・表現力】

『ひと粒の麦～ Moment ～』…さだまさしさんが，中村哲さんに（1.　　　　　）ために書いた歌

・中村さんは「100の診療所より1本の（2.　　　　　）を」というスローガンを掲げていた。
・（3.　　　　　）に知り合いがいたため，中村さんにいつか会えるだろうと思っていたが，
　会えないうちに亡くなってしまった。
・彼がアフガニスタンにまいた（4.　　　　　）は育ち続けると強く信じている。

B Key Sentences
重要文について理解しよう

Fill in the blanks and translate the following sentences.
【知識・技能】【思考力・判断力・表現力】

⑤ Nakamura worked there as a physician for over thirty years and maintained merely offering medical services was insufficient.

◆ there = in 1.＿＿＿＿＿＿＿＿＿＿＿＿＿＿
◆ maintainは，ここでは「…だと主張する」の意味で，maintain＋S＋Vの形になっている。
訳：＿＿＿＿＿＿＿＿＿＿＿＿＿＿＿＿＿＿＿＿＿＿＿＿＿＿＿＿＿
＿＿＿＿＿＿＿＿＿＿＿＿＿＿＿＿＿＿＿＿＿＿＿＿＿

⑮ Though I couldn't have a chance to talk with him directly, I feel as if he had helped me make this song.

◆ as if＋仮定法過去完了で，「まるで…であったかのように」の意味。
◆ help＋O＋C（＝原形不定詞）は「OがCするのを手伝う[助ける]」の意味。
訳：＿＿＿＿＿＿＿＿＿＿＿＿＿＿＿＿＿＿＿＿＿＿＿＿＿＿＿＿＿
＿＿＿＿＿＿＿＿＿＿＿＿＿＿＿＿＿＿＿＿＿＿＿＿＿

⑯ I strongly believe the seeds he sowed in Afghanistan will continue to grow.

◆ he sowed in Afghanistanは，後ろから 2.＿＿＿＿＿＿＿＿＿＿＿＿＿＿ を修飾している。
訳：＿＿＿＿＿＿＿＿＿＿＿＿＿＿＿＿＿＿＿＿＿＿＿＿＿＿＿＿＿
＿＿＿＿＿＿＿＿＿＿＿＿＿＿＿＿＿＿＿＿＿＿＿＿＿

🔊 意味のまとまりに注意して，本文全体を聞こう！

1 ① Food is important / for our lives. // ② It provides us / with energy and nutrition. // ③ However, / we have been facing many serious problems / related to food. //

2 ④ For example, / the Food and Agriculture Organization (FAO) shows / that more than 820 million people, / one in every nine / on earth, / are suffering from hunger. // ⑤ On the other hand, / the world's annual food waste / amounts to 1.3 billion tons. // ⑥ This is roughly a third of the total food production / in the world. // ⑦ In addition, / many studies report / that climate change has had negative effects / on crop quality. // ⑧ Moreover, / there is a growing need / to address the diversity / of dietary habits / such as vegetarianism and veganism. // ⑨ Shortages of human resources / in primary food-related industries / have also been a big challenge / for many years. //

3 ⑩ "Food technology," / known as "FoodTech" / in Japan, / may be one of the promising solutions / to many of these problems. // ⑪ It means applying science / to the production, / distribution, / preparation / and development / of food. // ⑫ It is expected / that the market size / of the FoodTech industry / will greatly increase / in the future. // (175 words)

New Words 新出単語の意味を調べよう		🔊 意味のまとまりに注意して，本文全体を音読しよう！	
nutrition 名 [njuːtríʃ(ə)n] B1	1.	hunger 名 [hʌ́ŋgər] B1	2.
roughly 副 [rʌ́fli] A2	3.	dietary 形 [dáɪətèri]	4.
vegetarianism 名 [vèdʒətéəriənìz(ə)m]	5.	veganism 名 [víːg(ə)nìz(ə)m]	6.

| primary 形 [práɪmèri] B2 | 7. | FoodTech [fú:dtèk] | フードテック |
| distribution 名 [dìstrɪbjú:ʃ(ə)n] B1 | 8. | preparation 名 [prèpəréɪʃ(ə)n] B1 | 9. |

Ⓐ Comprehension
パラグラフの要点を整理しよう
Fill in the blanks in Japanese.　【思考力・判断力・表現力】

食に関する問題	
飢餓	地球上の(1.　　　　　　)人に1人が飢餓に苦しんでいる。
食料廃棄	世界の年間食料廃棄量は(2.　　　　　　)トン(総生産量の約3分の1)。
食の多様化	ベジタリアンやヴィーガンへの対応が必要になっている。
生産者不足	食に関する産業での(3.　　　　　)が不足している。

➡ 「フードテック」(＝食品の生産, 流通, 調理, 開発に(4.　　　　　　)を応用すること)が解
決策となりうる。

Ⓑ Key Sentences
重要文について理解しよう
Fill in the blanks and translate the following sentences.
【知識・技能】【思考力・判断力・表現力】

④ **For example, the Food and Agriculture Organization (FAO) shows that
more than 820 million people, one in every nine on earth, are suffering
from hunger.**

◆ more than 820 million people と one in every nine on earth が同格の関係になっている。

訳:

⑥ **This is roughly a third of the total food production in the world.**

◆ This は前文の 1.＿＿＿＿＿＿＿＿ を指す。

訳:

⑫ **It is expected that the market size of the FoodTech industry will greatly
increase in the future.**

◆ It is expected that ... は「…ということが予想される」という意味。

訳:

🔊 意味のまとまりに注意して，本文全体を聞こう！

4 [1]Food technology is utilized / in food production / in many ways. // [2]First, / there is now a variety of agricultural machinery. // [3]For example, / drones are used / to spray crops / with agricultural chemicals. // [4]Remotely operated farm tractors / cultivate land. // [5]Also, / some robots / with artificial intelligence / harvest crops / by judging from their color or shape. // [6]These kinds of technology / help solve the problem / of labor shortages / in food production industries. //

5 [7]Second, / so-called "plant factories" / are now in operation / to grow food. // [8]They do not need vast land or sunlight. // [9]They are not influenced / by the weather, / either. // [10]LED light, / CO_2 concentration / and temperature / in plant factories / are automatically controlled / for photosynthesis. // [11]Plant factories are an example / of ways / to deal with the problem / of climate change. //

6 [12]Food technology is also used / in food distribution. // [13]For instance, / restaurants can reduce food waste / by registering for services / on the Internet. // [14]One service helps restaurants / sell their surplus food / to general customers / at low prices. // [15]Such services directly connect food / with consumers / on the Internet. // [16]They are called "D2C" (direct-to-consumer) business models / and are only possible / through technology. // (181 words)

🔊 意味のまとまりに注意して，本文全体を音読しよう！

New Words 新出単語の意味を調べよう			
utilize 動 [júːt(ə)làɪz] B2	1.	machinery 名 [məʃíːn(ə)ri]	2.
spray 動 [spréɪ] B2	3.	chemical 名 [kémɪk(ə)l] B1	4.

operate 動 [á(ː)pərèɪt] A2	5.	tractor 名 [trǽktər]	6.
vast 形 [vǽst] B1	7.	concentration 名 [kà(ː)ns(ə)ntréɪʃ(ə)n] B1	8.
temperature 名 [témp(ə)rətʃər] A2	9.	automatically 副 [ɔ̀ːtəmǽtɪk(ə)li] A2	10.
photosynthesis 名 [fòʊtoʊsínθəsɪs]	11.		

A Comprehension
パラグラフの要点を整理しよう

Fill in the blanks in Japanese.　　　【思考力・判断力・表現力】

食品の生産におけるフードテックの活用	
①農業機械	ドローンによる（1.　　　　　　　）散布, 遠隔操作のトラクター, 人工知能搭載ロボットによる収穫。➡（2.　　　　　　　）の解決
②植物工場	広大な土地や日光が不要で,（3.　　　　　　　）に左右されない。➡気候変動問題への対策
食品の流通におけるフードテックの活用	
D2Cビジネスモデルを利用した（4.　　　　　　　）削減のためのサービス	

B Key Sentences
重要文について理解しよう

Fill in the blanks and translate the following sentences.
【知識・技能】【思考力・判断力・表現力】

⑤ Also, <u>some robots with artificial intelligence</u> <u>harvest</u> <u>crops</u> by judging
　　　　　　　　　　　　　S　　　　　　　　　　　　　　　　V　　　O
from their color or shape.

◆ S＋V＋Oの構造になっている。harvestは「…を収穫する」という意味の他動詞。

訳：＿＿＿＿＿＿＿＿＿＿＿＿＿＿＿＿＿＿＿＿＿＿＿＿＿＿＿＿＿＿＿＿

⑩ LED light, CO_2 concentration and temperature in plant factories are automatically controlled for photosynthesis.

◆ LED light, ... plant factoriesまでが主語。動詞はare controlledで, 受け身になっている。

訳：＿＿＿＿＿＿＿＿＿＿＿＿＿＿＿＿＿＿＿＿＿＿＿＿＿＿＿＿＿＿＿＿

⑯ They are called "D2C" (direct-to-consumer) business models and are only possible through technology.

◆ 2つの動詞are calledと1.＿＿＿＿＿＿＿＿が並列されている。

訳：＿＿＿＿＿＿＿＿＿＿＿＿＿＿＿＿＿＿＿＿＿＿＿＿＿＿＿＿＿＿＿＿

🔊 意味のまとまりに注意して，本文全体を聞こう！

7 ①Food technology also contributes / to food preparation. // ②Cooking methods / based on food technology / have been becoming popular recently. // ③For example, / you can transform cooking ingredients / into a mousse-formed substance / by adding CO_2. // ④This creates different textures. // ⑤You can also freeze cooking ingredients instantly / with liquid nitrogen / to preserve their flavor and freshness. //

8 ⑥The "smart kitchen" still sounds unfamiliar, / but it may change the way / we cook / at home / in the near future. // ⑦This applies "IoT" (Internet of Things) / to cooking. // ⑧It connects recipes, / grocery shopping / and food preparation. // ⑨First, / you select your favorite recipe / for your meal / on a special app / in your smartphone. // ⑩Next, / you order the ingredients / by tapping on them. // ⑪Then, / after the ingredients are delivered, / the smart kitchen will start / to help you cook / by controlling your kitchen appliances. // ⑫As a result, / the smart kitchen can gather various data / such as when and what you eat. // ⑬With such personal data, / it will be able to help design an ideal diet. //

9 ⑭As mentioned above, / food technology is utilized / in food preparation / in many ways. // ⑮It will help people / enjoy making and eating their meals, / and become healthier. // (190 words)

🔊 意味のまとまりに注意して，本文全体を音読しよう！

New Words 新出単語の意味を調べよう

transform 動 [trænsfɔ́ːrm] B1	1.	mousse 名 [múːs]	2.
substance 名 [sʌ́bst(ə)ns] B2	3.	texture 名 [tékstʃər]	4.
freeze 動 [fríːz] A2	5.	instantly 副 [ínst(ə)ntli] B2	6.
liquid 形 [líkwɪd] B1	7.	nitrogen 名 [náɪtrədʒ(ə)n]	8.
flavor 名 [fléɪvər] B1	9.	freshness 名 [fréʃnəs]	10.

unfamiliar 形 [ʌ̀nfəmíljər] B2	11.	grocery 名 [gróus(ə)ri]	12.
app 名 [ǽp]	13.	diet 名 [dáɪət] A2	14.
mention 動 [ménʃ(ə)n] B1	15.		

A **Comprehension**
パラグラフの要点を整理しよう
Fill in the blanks in Japanese.　　　　【思考力・判断力・表現力】

食品の調理におけるフードテックの活用
・二酸化炭素を加えて素材を(1.　　　　　　)状に。➡多様な食感を生み出す
・(2.　　　　　　　)を用いて素材を急速冷凍。➡風味と鮮度の保持
・スマートキッチン…①アプリで好きな(3.　　　　　　)を選択，②材料を注文，③スマートキッチンがキッチン家電を制御し，調理を手伝う。
➡さまざまな(4.　　　　　)を収集し，理想的な食生活を設計

B **Key Sentences**
重要文について理解しよう
Fill in the blanks and translate the following sentences.
【知識・技能】【思考力・判断力・表現力】

② Cooking methods based on food technology have been becoming popular
S　　　　　　　　　　　　　　　　　　　　　　　V　　　　　　　C
recently.

◆ S＋V＋Cの文。主語のCooking methodsは，過去分詞のbased ... によって後置修飾されている。

◆ have been becomingは現在完了進行形で継続を表す。

訳：_____

⑫ As a result, the smart kitchen can gather various data such as when and
what you eat.

◆ such as以下は直前のvarious dataの具体例を表している。when and what you eatは間接疑問文。

訳：_____

⑮ It will help people enjoy making and eating their meals, and become
healthier.

◆ It＝ 1._____

◆ help＋O＋C（＝原形不定詞）の構文になっている。2._____ と 3._____ の２つの
原形不定詞が並列されている。

訳：_____

教科書 p.156-157

🔊 意味のまとまりに注意して，本文全体を聞こう！

A   Imitation meat / and cultured meat //

①Imitation meat is a meat-like product / produced from plants. // ②It is mainly made / from soybeans, / wheat, / peas / and so on. // ③It can address dietary diversity / such as vegetarianism and veganism. // ④Cultured meat is produced / by culturing the cells / of animals / instead of killing them. // ⑤Both kinds of meat / taste just like real meat, / and they may be considered / better than conventional meat / in terms of ethical, / health, / environmental, / cultural / and economic aspects. //

B   Insect food //

⑥Some insects are edible / and high in protein. // ⑦Actually, / they have been consumed / as food / in some countries / for many years. // ⑧Popular species are grasshoppers, / crickets, / beetles, / bees, / and others. // ⑨Recently, / they are being processed / with technology / and made into various useful forms / such as powders, / pastes, / liquids / and oils. // ⑩Insect food can be mass-produced sustainably / and is expected / to be a solution / to food crises and hunger. //

C   Meal replacement //

⑪Meal replacement refers to pre-packaged food meals. // ⑫It is full of nutrients / such as proteins, / fats, / fiber, / vitamins, / minerals / and carbohydrates. // ⑬It comes in various forms / such as powders, / bars, / drinks, / etc. // ⑭Meal replacement products / are convenient alternatives / for healthy and low-calorie meals. //　(183 words)　🔊 意味のまとまりに注意して，本文全体を音読しよう！

New Words 新出単語の意味を調べよう			
webpage 名 [wébpèɪdʒ] A2	1.	cultured 形 [kʌ́ltʃərd]	2.
soybean 名 [sɔ́ɪbìːn] B2	3.	pea 名 [píː] A2	4.

conventional 形 [kənvénʃ(ə)n(ə)l] B2	5.	edible 形 [édəb(ə)l]	6.
protein 名 [próʊtiːn]	7.	consume 動 [kənsúːm] B1	8.
cricket 名 [kríkət]	9.	beetle 名 [bíːt(ə)l]	10.
paste 名 [péɪst]	11.	crisis 名 [kráɪsɪs] B1	12.
replacement 名 [rɪpléɪsmənt] B2	13.	packaged 形 [pǽkɪdʒd]	14.
nutrient 名 [njúːtriənt] B1	15.	carbohydrate 名 [kɑ̀ːrboʊháɪdreɪt]	16.
etc. 名 [etsét(ə)rə]	17.	alternative 名 [ɔːltə́ːrnətɪv] B1	18.

A Comprehension
パラグラフの要点を整理しよう
Fill in the blanks in Japanese.　【思考力・判断力・表現力】

食品の開発におけるフードテックの活用	
代替肉 培養肉	代替肉：(1.　　　　　　　)，小麦，エンドウ豆が原料。 培養肉：動物の(2.　　　　　　)を培養して作る。 ➡食の多様性に対応でき，倫理，健康，環境，文化，経済面で優れている。
昆虫食	バッタやコオロギなどの昆虫を，粉末やペースト，液体，油などに加工。 ➡持続的に(3.　　　　　　)が可能で，食料危機や飢餓の解決策となりうる。
完全食	豊富な栄養素を含み，粉末やバー，飲み物などの食品。 ➡健康的で低(4.　　　　　　)な食事として便利な代替品。

B Key Sentences
重要文について理解しよう
Fill in the blanks and translate the following sentences.
　【知識・技能】【思考力・判断力・表現力】

⑦ **Actually, they have been consumed as food in some countries for many years.**

◆ they = some 1.＿＿＿＿＿＿＿＿＿

訳：..

⑩ **Insect food can be mass-produced sustainably and is expected to be a solution to food crises and hunger.**

◆ 主語 Insect food に対して2つの動詞句が並列されていて，どちらも受け身の形になっている。

訳：..
....

🔊 意味のまとまりに注意して，本文全体を聞こう！

①Now, / let me give you three examples / of global issues / facing the world today. // ②First, / we often hear news / like "We had the most devastating flood / in a century." // ③In fact, / climate change has become so serious / that it can be referred to / as the "climate crisis." // ④Second, / unfortunately, / hunger and poverty / in developing countries / still remain as huge barriers / to sustainable development. // ⑤According to the United Nations, / every year / about six million children / die from hunger and poor nutrition. // ⑥The third example is the issue of education. // ⑦We have to face the fact / that hundreds of millions of children / around the world / are unable to attend school. //

⑧As you know, / there is no time / to lose / in tackling these global issues. // ⑨That's why the UN has adopted the 17 Sustainable Development Goals / — the SDGs. // ⑩They are a blueprint / for peace and prosperity / for people and the planet, / now and into the future. // ⑪They are an urgent call / to action / by all countries / in a global partnership. //

⑫Now is the time / to consider what we can do / as individuals. // ⑬It is not enough / for us / to understand what the issues are. // ⑭We must transform the world / through our daily actions. // (200 words)

🔊 意味のまとまりに注意して，本文全体を音読しよう！

New Words 新出単語の意味を調べよう			
poverty 名 [pá(:)vərti] B1	1.	blueprint 名 [blú:prìnt]	2.
prosperity 名 [prɑ(:)spérəti] B1	3.	partnership 名 [pá:rtnərʃìp] B2	4.

Ⓐ Comprehension
パラグラフの要点を整理しよう

Fill in the blanks in Japanese.

【思考力・判断力・表現力】

世界の諸問題	
①気候変動	「気候(1.　　　　　　)」と称されるほど深刻化している。
②飢餓と貧困	毎年約600万人の子供たちが飢えや(2.　　　　　　)で亡くなっている。
③教育問題	世界では何億人もの子供たちが学校に通えていない。
➡国連が17の(3.　　　　　　)な開発目標(SDGs)を採択。	
私たち一人ひとりが(4.　　　　　　)の行動を通して世界を変えていかなければならない。	

Ⓑ Key Sentences
重要文について理解しよう

Fill in the blanks and translate the following sentences.

【知識・技能】【思考力・判断力・表現力】

③ In fact, climate change has become so serious that it can be referred to as the "climate crisis."

◆ so … that ～は「とても…なので～，～するほど…」の意味。

◆ A is referred to as Bは refer to A as B「AをBと呼ぶ」の受動態で，「AはBと呼ばれる」の意味。

訳：_____

_____

⑦ We have to face the fact that hundreds of millions of children around the world are unable to attend school.

◆ thatは「…という～」という同格を表す接続詞。the fact that … で「…という事実」の意味。

◆ be unable to ～は「～することができない」(= 1._____ ～)

訳：_____

_____

⑩ They are a blueprint for peace and prosperity for people and the planet, now and into the future.

◆ 1つ目のandはpeaceと 2._____ を，2つ目のandはpeopleと the planetを，3つ目のandは 3._____ と into the futureを結びつけている。

訳：_____

_____

教科書 p.168-169

🔊 意味のまとまりに注意して，本文全体を聞こう！

①I'd like to talk about SDG Goal 4, / "Quality Education." // ②I think / education is the most important thing / to improve our society. // ③This SDG's goal is / to make sure / that everyone can equally get a good education. // ④Education enables us / to live on our own / and escape poverty. // ⑤I have learned / that a large number of children / around the world / cannot attend school. // ⑥I'm very shocked / to know this reality. // ⑦I'm wondering what we can do / as individuals. //

⑧I want to introduce the "World TERAKOYA Movement (WTM)." // ⑨In 1989, / a Japanese NGO started it / as an international cooperation program / for education. // ⑩The main objective / of the WTM / is to provide illiterate adults and out-of-school children / with opportunities / to receive an education. // ⑪I am impressed / by the goal / of the WTM: / to end the cycle / of poverty and illiteracy. //

⑫On its website, / I heard a TERAKOYA student say, / "I'm very happy / that I was able to write my name / for the first time / in my life." // ⑬My future dream is / to be a teacher. // ⑭I hope to teach children / living in harsh conditions / like him / someday. // (185 words)

New Words 新出単語の意味を調べよう		🔊 意味のまとまりに注意して，本文全体を音読しよう！	
objective 名 [əbdʒéktɪv] B1	1.	illiterate 形 [ɪlít(ə)rət]	2.
cycle 名 [sáɪk(ə)l] B1	3.	illiteracy 名 [ɪlít(ə)rəsi]	4.
harsh 形 [háːrʃ]	5.		

A Comprehension
パラグラフの要点を整理しよう
Fill in the blanks in Japanese.
【思考力・判断力・表現力】

SDGsの目標4：「質の高い教育をみんなに」	
教育を受けることで，生きていく力を身につけ，（1.　　　　　　　　）から抜け出すことができる。	
具体的取り組み： 世界寺子屋運動	…1989年に日本の（2.　　　　　　　）が始めた教育の国際協力プログラム。 （3.　　　　　　　）のできない大人や学校に通っていない子供たちに教育を受ける機会を提供し，（4.　　　　　　　）と非識字の連鎖を断ち切ることを目的としている。

B Key Sentences
重要文について理解しよう
Fill in the blanks and translate the following sentences.
【知識・技能】【思考力・判断力・表現力】

③ <u>This SDG's goal</u> <u>is</u> <u>to make sure that everyone can equally get a good</u>
　　　 S　　　　　 V　　　　　　　　　　　　　　　　C

<u>education.</u>

◆ This SDG's goal = SDG Goal 4, "1.＿＿＿＿＿＿＿＿＿＿＿＿＿"

◆ S＋V＋Cの文。補語になっているto make …は不定詞の名詞用法。

訳：＿＿＿＿＿＿＿＿＿＿＿＿＿＿＿＿＿＿＿＿＿＿＿＿＿＿＿＿＿＿
　　＿＿＿＿＿＿＿＿＿＿＿＿＿＿＿＿＿＿＿＿＿＿＿＿＿＿＿＿＿＿

④ **Education enables us to live on our own and escape poverty.**

◆ enable … to ～は「…が～することを可能にする」という意味。

訳：＿＿＿＿＿＿＿＿＿＿＿＿＿＿＿＿＿＿＿＿＿＿＿＿＿＿＿＿＿＿

⑩ <u>The main objective of the WTM</u> <u>is</u> <u>to provide illiterate adults and out-of-</u>
　　　　　　 S　　　　　　　　 V　　　　　　　 C

<u>school children with opportunities to receive an education.</u>

◆ S＋V＋Cの文。補語になっているto provide …は不定詞の名詞用法。

◆ provide A with Bで「AにBを供給する」の意味。（＝ provide B for [to] A）

訳：＿＿＿＿＿＿＿＿＿＿＿＿＿＿＿＿＿＿＿＿＿＿＿＿＿＿＿＿＿＿
　　＿＿＿＿＿＿＿＿＿＿＿＿＿＿＿＿＿＿＿＿＿＿＿＿＿＿＿＿＿＿

⑪ **I am impressed by the goal of the WTM: to end the cycle of poverty and**
　 illiteracy.

◆ コロン以下は2.＿＿＿＿＿＿＿＿＿＿＿＿＿＿＿＿＿＿の具体的な内容を表している。

訳：＿＿＿＿＿＿＿＿＿＿＿＿＿＿＿＿＿＿＿＿＿＿＿＿＿＿＿＿＿＿
　　＿＿＿＿＿＿＿＿＿＿＿＿＿＿＿＿＿＿＿＿＿＿＿＿＿＿＿＿＿＿

教科書 p.170-171

🔊 意味のまとまりに注意して，本文全体を聞こう！

①What I am most interested in / is SDG Goal 7. // ②Its purpose is to provide people / with affordable, reliable, sustainable and clean energy. // ③For many years, / fossil fuels have been the major energy resource. // ④But / burning fossil fuels / has been producing large amounts of greenhouse gases. // ⑤They have caused climate change / and have had harmful impacts / on the environment. //

⑥Let me tell you about Norway. // ⑦Surprisingly, / in Norway, / almost 100% of all electricity production / comes from renewables, / for the most part hydropower. // ⑧Norway's energy policy may be a special case, / but it's a good model / for our country. // ⑨As you know, / Japan is trying to increase the use of renewables, / but their percentage will only increase / from 18% / to over 30% / by 2030. //

⑩Don't you think / it is time / to take urgent action / to shift from fossil fuels / to renewables? // ⑪However, / the world, / especially many developing countries, / will need more and more energy / to develop their economies. // ⑫It is a great challenge / to meet all the potential energy needs / only by using clean energy sources. // ⑬No matter how difficult it is, / we must do it / to preserve the earth / for future generations. // (192 words)

🔊 意味のまとまりに注意して，本文全体を音読しよう！

New Words 新出単語の意味を調べよう

reliable 形 [rɪláɪəb(ə)l] B1	1.	fossil 形 [fá(:)s(ə)l]	2.
fuel 名 [fjúːəl] B1	3.	greenhouse 名 [gríːnhàus] B1	4.

| renewable 名
[rɪnjúːəb(ə)l] | 5. | hydropower 名
[háɪdrəpàʊər] | 6. |
| shift 動 [ʃíft] B1 | 7. | source 名 [sɔ́ːrs] A2 | 8. |

A Comprehension
パラグラフの要点を整理しよう
Fill in the blanks in Japanese. 【思考力・判断力・表現力】

SDGsの目標7：「エネルギーをみんなに そしてクリーンに」	
長年依存してきた(1.　　　　　)から脱却し，(2.　　　　　)で信頼できる，持続可能でクリーンなエネルギーを人々に提供する。	
ノルウェーの エネルギー事情	電力のほぼ100％が(3.　　　　　)エネルギーによって発電されており，そのほとんどが水力発電による。
日本の エネルギー事情	現状，日本の再生可能エネルギーの利用は(4.　　　　　)％にすぎず，2030年までの目標値も30％超でしかない。

B Key Sentences
重要文について理解しよう
Fill in the blanks and translate the following sentences.
【知識・技能】【思考力・判断力・表現力】

⑦ Surprisingly, in Norway, almost 100% of all electricity production comes from renewables, for the most part hydropower.

◆ surprisinglyは「驚くことに，意外にも」という意味の文修飾副詞である。

訳：

⑫ It is a great challenge to meet all the potential energy needs only by using clean energy sources.

◆ It is ... to ～の構文。Itは形式主語で，to以下の内容を指す。

訳：

⑬ No matter how difficult it is, we must do it to preserve the earth for future generations.

◆ no matter how ...は「(たとえ)どんなに…でも」という意味。

◆ to preserveは「～するために」という目的を表す不定詞の副詞用法。

訳：

教科書 p.172-173

🔊 意味のまとまりに注意して，本文全体を聞こう！

①I'd like to take up SDG Goal 1 / and SDG Goal 3. // ②SDG Goal 1, / "No Poverty," / is to end poverty / in all its forms / everywhere / by 2030. // ③SDG Goal 3, / "Good Health and Well-being," / aims to ensure healthy lives / and promote well-being / for all people / of all ages. //

④SDG Goals 1 and 3 / are strongly interconnected. // ⑤In other words, / "No Poverty" is closely linked / to good health. // ⑥In fact, / people living in extreme poverty / cannot fulfill their most basic needs / like good health. // ⑦Have you ever heard / of "Doctors Without Borders"? // ⑧It is an international medical humanitarian organization / founded / in 1971 / in Paris. // ⑨It provides basic medical care / for people / affected by war, / epidemics / or disasters. // ⑩I am impressed / that it is trying to realize SDG Goals 1 and 3. //

⑪My future dream, / if possible, / is to work / as a volunteer / for "Doctors Without Borders." // ⑫The organization is made up of people / with diverse backgrounds / from all over the world. // ⑬The experience / of working with such people / would definitely be a precious opportunity / for me, / and I would be happy / to contribute to the achievement / of the goals / of the SDGs. //

(193 words) 🔊 意味のまとまりに注意して，本文全体を音読しよう！

New Words 新出単語の意味を調べよう			
healthcare 名 [hélθkèər] B2	1.	ensure 動 [ɪnʃúər] B1	2.
interconnect 動 [ìntərkənékt]	3.	extreme 形 [ɪkstríːm] B1	4.

fulfill 動 [fʊlfíl] B2	5.	border 名 [bɔ́ːrdər] B1	6.
epidemic 名 [èpɪdémɪk]	7.	definitely 副 [déf(ə)nətli] B1	8.

A Comprehension
パラグラフの要点を整理しよう

Fill in the blanks in Japanese.　　　【思考力・判断力・表現力】

SDGsの目標1：「貧困をなくそう」		
2030年までに，あらゆる場所であらゆる形態の(1.　　　　　)を終わらせる。		
SDGsの目標3：「すべての人に健康と福祉を」		
すべての人々に(2.　　　　　)な生活を確保し，幸福を促進する。		
具体的取り組み：「国境なき医師団」	…1971年にパリで設立された国際的な医療人道支援団体。(3.　　　　　)や疫病，災害に苦しむ人々に(4.　　　　　)を提供している。	

B Key Sentences
重要文について理解しよう

Fill in the blanks and translate the following sentences.
　　　【知識・技能】【思考力・判断力・表現力】

③ SDG Goal 3, "**Good Health and Well-being**," aims to ensure healthy lives and promote well-being for all people of all ages.

◆ SDG Goal 3と "Good Health and Well-being" は同格の関係になっている。

◆ andはensure healthy livesと 1.　　　　　　　　　　を並列に結んでいる。

訳 :

⑥ In fact, people living in extreme poverty cannot fulfill their most basic needs like good health.

◆ living in extreme povertyがpeopleを修飾しており，この部分全体が主語になっている。

◆ likeは「…のような」という意味の前置詞で, like以下がtheir most basic needsの具体例を表している。

訳 :

⑫ The organization is made up of people with diverse backgrounds from all over the world.

◆ be made up of ... は「…で構成されている」という意味。

◆ with diverse backgroundsとfrom all over the worldの2つの前置詞句がpeopleを修飾している。

訳 :